"Have you ever met someone who could walk into a room filled with people from all walks of life and immediately make everyone feel like they just gained a new best friend? I never had until I met Kimi. There's something uniquely special about Kimi's ability to build relationships and genuinely connect with people. I've heard the expression, 'People don't care how much you know until they know how much you care,' and that quote encapsulates Kimi's approach to friendships, business partnerships, acquaintances, and everything in between. She's unbelievably well-accomplished yet humble, and she doesn't have an inauthentic bone in her body. She truly cares, and everyone that I've had the privilege of introducing to her over the last decade has immediately felt the same way."

—Chris Pemberton
Language Expert, Entrepreneur

"Kimi is one of the strongest, most driven, competitive, resilient, and people-oriented individuals I know. When we started working together, she was a recent Air Force veteran and MBA graduate, a successful government employee, a new mother, and an aspiring entrepreneur. When her transition to full-time entrepreneurship didn't go as planned, she was able to step back, evaluate the situation objectively, then develop and execute solutions to make it work anyway. In situations where most people tend to get stuck, Kimi keeps moving forward. Experiencing, enduring, and ultimately overcoming difficult and painful challenges is what drives her passion for helping others. Her ability to share and communicate her experiences are key factors that make her so relatable to other people. No matter how many things she has on her plate, she always manages to juggle it all while still making people feel valued and important."

—Trisha Verzera
Network Marketing Coach

"Kim O'Neill is one of the realest people I know. True to the core, she is a leader's leader who has the courage to own it when she's not living up to her ability. Leading by example makes Kim who she is as a leader, friend, wife, mother, and sister. She consistently makes hard choices to fix what isn't working and then uses it to help others do the same. It's been a blessing and inspiration having her challenge me to live my best life."

—Mikki Gayle
Entrepreneur

"I've known Kimi for the last twenty-plus years and have been witness to every one of her evolutions. To say that she is focused and determined to reach her goals is an understatement. Although she's gone through many hard times, she's come through to the other side stronger, wiser, and more compassionate. Kimi's resiliency is complemented by a titanium will, allowing her to adapt and crush any challenge. She's a conqueror."

—Sandra Serrano
Air Force (Ret.)

"Making the transition from employee to entrepreneur is not easy, but Kim not only accepted the challenge, but she also accomplished it like a boss. Her persistence and determination to make a difference come from a genuine place in her heart. She has proven time and time again that we are reflections of how we handle adversity. Kim has successfully combined her personal and professional life to create a beautiful balance. Seeing someone pursue their passion is always inspiring, and Kim continues to inspire."

—Cyndi Po
Executive Coaching

"I have never met anyone more authentic than Kimi O'Neill. Finding someone so passionate and "matter-of-fact" was exactly what I needed to take me from where I was to where I deserved to be! Since 2015, I have watched her grow not only professionally and as an amazing mother but also in her willingness to include everyone as if they are family. With Kimi, there's no judgment, and everyone counts."

—Jason A. Elliot I, MS, PA-C

"There isn't enough room in an ENTIRE book to depict the incredible woman Kimi is today. There are certain things in life that 99% of people just won't do, overcome, or even try. Kimi is a phenomenon when it comes to her drive and commitment to not only her success but also to those around her. She has helped me succeed in many areas of my own life. We have worked together on numerous endeavors, and there hasn't been a single one where she did not succeed because she doesn't understand the word 'quit!' Family, friends, business—there's just no quit. Giving back and helping others—still no quit. Kimi doesn't define success by her own accomplishments; she attributes it to how successful she helps those around her become. There is no comparison to how much better this world is, as long as Kimi O'Neill is in it."

—Kasey Kahl
Business Owner, CEO

"I was nine years old, wandering around the playground when this girl asked me if I wanted to play kickball. I was so excited that someone wanted to do something with me that I liked. I knew at that moment Kim would forever be one of my people. Our whole lives, she has challenged me to do and be better. She asks the tough questions that make you truly evaluate the 'why' behind your thoughts and actions. Kim has a way of making you dig deeper than you would have thought possible. I've watched her diligently work towards her own goals, overcome obstacles with grace, and become the consummate leader. To this day, she is one of the most genuine and humble people I know. If given the opportunity to learn from Kim, I encourage you to take it. Your life may just be better for it."

—Charity Glenn
Flight Nurse

BREAKTHROUGH
LEADERSHIP

with KIMBERLY O'NEILL

ALSO FEATURING
OTHER TOP AUTHORS

© 2021 Success Publishing

Success Publishing, LLC
P.O. Box 703536
Dallas, Texas 75370 USA

questions@mattmorris.com

Table of Contents

CHAPTER 1

Break The Mold

By Kimberly O'Neill

The most important "job" I find myself fortunate enough to have is that of being a parent. I'm a mom, and the majority of my decisions now reflect that role and my desire to do it well. I'm also an overachiever. I was always an overachiever. When it came to sports, I excelled. When it came to the military, I excelled. When it came to graduate school, I excelled. Pretty much every goal I set for myself, I achieved and excelled. But I rarely took time to celebrate the wins and consistently looked for the next goal. Something was always missing.

I still had a voice in the back of my mind saying, "You have to do more! You aren't doing enough! And what you are doing isn't good enough! Be better! Do more! You aren't there yet! It's not enough!" I also had a strong desire to be liked and accepted, and this voice would tell me things like, "You just don't fit in. You aren't like everyone else. You have to change for people to like you because you aren't thin enough, fit enough, smart enough, interesting enough, fun enough, and likable enough. You just aren't enough. Do more. Be more." I don't know where this voice came from or why it plagued me virtually my entire life, but I know I'm not alone.

I also can pinpoint the events that led me to really challenge this voice and reach a point where I am my own voice, where I write my own script, where I don't need the approval of others, and where I really do love myself for who I am, where I've been, and who I am becoming. It definitely didn't happen overnight. In fact, I have been a work in progress for more than a decade, with the real fruits of my labor finally coming into bloom since around 2020.

In 2004, I found out I was pregnant. I was in the middle of school for my new career as an officer in the Air Force, which wasn't ideal because the training was demanding. A few weeks in, I underwent emergency surgery to save my life when the pregnancy caused my fallopian tube to rupture. I lost the baby and half of my fertility in the blink of an eye.

While nobody said I couldn't feel grief for the trauma or that I couldn't mourn the loss of my child, I worried that allowing myself to feel it would lead to a breakdown and that a breakdown—given the requirements of my field—could potentially end my career. So, I focused on my training so intently that I graduated #1 in my class. Fast forward to my first duty assignment, I was blessed with a second chance at pregnancy, only to be devastated again. This time, I focused on work and was on rotation for deployment in a matter of weeks.

These events were undoubtedly the catalyst for what came next. It wasn't until I was out of the military, remarried, and trying to conceive again that I recognized the damage, danger, and lingering pain that was never addressed.

Broken. Unworthy. Failure. Not enough. These are just a few of the pervasive thoughts that preceded what I would call an absolute breakdown and tearing apart of who I thought I was, followed by choices, risky behaviors, and self-sabotage to a level that can only be described as perhaps an attempt to live up to the useless and broken unworthiness I felt inside of myself.

I had decided that doing all the right things and being excellent didn't matter. So, I did things that were in stark contrast to who I was at the core—things that would allow me to justify the shame and disappointment I felt in myself in a way that put me in control. I denied my integrity as if it were a way to punish myself for being inadequate. This was hands down the most difficult, uncomfortable, and borderline hopeless time I can remember ever experiencing in my life.

Fast forward to the present day, and I will tell you that I have given birth to two incredible, beautiful miracle children who are my life, heart, and soul. My daughter, in no uncertain terms, saved my life. I was in a downward spiral of drinking and partying, and I was in a very toxic relationship that perpetuated the self-destructive cycle. I was running.

I had convinced myself that my choices up to that point got me exactly what I deserved and that I was unworthy of any real kind of healthy love. She was unplanned and unexpected and truly the gift that drove me to get my life together again.

Focusing on her, my own fog started to clear, and I started remembering who I was and who I wanted to be. I started making decisions that brought me more in line with my integrity. I landed a government job, bought us a house, and ended my toxic relationship with her father. I wasn't completely there yet, but I was getting there.

Eventually, I remarried. Fertility issues struck again, but this time, when the self-talk threatened to take a turn for the worst, I sought help to avoid the catastrophic shutdown that I experienced before. Recognizing and honoring that need was the first step to a long road of healing and growth.

After seven years, three losses, two more emergent surgeries, and multiple failed attempts with in-vitro fertilization, I decided continuing to try was no longer healthy for me. As irrational as I knew it was, feelings of inadequacy and the perception that I was broken or damaged made me feel less of a woman and undeserving of happiness. I was losing myself, and enough was enough.

Overachievers like to be in control, but this was something I could not control. So, I would distract myself with work or take more classes—things that would help me feel accomplished. After a few years, my love for my work had lost its luster when the environment became very toxic. I found myself avoiding interaction as much as possible. I would show up, shut my door, and keep to myself. At the end of the day, I would wind down with a glass of wine, or sometimes, a bottle. I felt lonely and lost.

What was the point? I felt no sense of purpose anymore. I felt like I was just going through the motions of life and certainly was not as present as I could have been at home as a result. Something was missing. Again.

I wanted to spend more time with my family. I wanted to have more freedom in my days. I hated punching a clock. I felt like my life was wasting away and passing me by while I sat in that office. But it was a "good" job, with stability, benefits, and opportunities for growth, right? I should feel grateful, not resistant, right? What was wrong with me?

Then in 2016, I attended a training where I learned the term "cognitive dissonance," which refers to the state of discomfort felt when two or more modes of thought contradict each other. This created a major epiphany for me, and this is where my life took a major warp speed turn for the better.

I had a good job, but it could never give me the life I knew I wanted. It provided stability but not freedom. It provided an opportunity but not the kind I wanted. I had ideas I wanted to pursue, but they conflicted with my career. I sat in that training, and the idea hit me like a tidal wave: "I have to quit my job. I'm going to quit my job!"

Now, I don't recommend making rash life decisions! But to be honest, I had written my resignation letter two years prior. I just hadn't followed through with it! I finally had the courage to execute the action! I was going to quit my job and pursue my entrepreneurial endeavors. I let go of that toxic relationship, too, and I felt a million times lighter.

Less than a month later, I was pregnant with my son: no intervention, no treatments, no medication, and no issues. At forty-one years old, I had a miracle baby boy who has been my heart and soul ever since. The gift of my children, combined with my realization that I get to create my own destiny, led to even more personal development, which in turn led to more opportunities.

I had an unquenchable thirst for knowledge. I read dozens of books on self-awareness, parenting, childhood development, conscious parenting, the subconscious mind, body language, intuition, energy, and being present. I went to school for life coaching and neuro linguistic programming. I attended personal development seminars, and I was eventually offered a position as a contract leadership development trainer, where I got to choose my own schedule and was well-compensated for my time and knowledge.

Then, in 2020, I said goodbye to my final toxic relationship, alcohol. It started with a thirty-day alcohol experiment to evaluate and challenge my thought processes and behaviors around alcohol. About two weeks into the experiment, my mindset changed so much that I literally had no desire to ever consume alcohol again. I not only didn't want it, but I became repelled by the thought of it. The last thing I ever want my kids to feel is that mommy needs wine to deal with being their mom.

I started to save the money I would've been spending on wine. I thought I'd do something nice for myself at the end of the thirty days, but 500+ days later, I had saved $3,696. It was time to do something epic to celebrate. So, I gathered up my kids, and we hit the road for a cross-country adventure! We spent two full weeks traveling, camping, exploring, laughing, and experiencing our world in ways we'd not done before. Our time was flexible, as were our destinations. Our only objectives were freedom and adventure.

Success looks different to different people. But for me, I'm literally living the dream. I've always been someone who would see challenges and be of the FITFO mindset. FITFO to me meant "Figure It the F*&S Out!" Stop complaining, stop whining, stop focusing on the obstacles, and just figure out how to get it done. But now, more often than not, it means "Focus Inward To Find Opportunity."

Focus inward, because nobody knows what is best for us more than ourselves. If we listen for it, look for it, and feel for it, we know what decisions are right for us. They may not make sense to other people, and that's okay. It involves letting go of any expectations we think other people have of us, breaking out of the mold of living life in a prescribed fashion, and confidently following our own path.

It's asking yourself questions like, "How is this serving me? What might serve me better? What kind of internal dialogue am I having about this? Do I like the way this script is going, or should I change it? What would I rather hear? Does this feel authentic? Am I experiencing cognitive dissonance? If so, why? What's off? What would be more in line with me? What is the reality of this situation if I remove all judgment?"

This approach has enabled me to eliminate toxicity from my life. It helped me break the mold of who I thought I should be, allowing me to embrace who I am and who I want to be.

Focus inward, because being self-aware and authentic is key to everything. We cannot lead anyone until we can lead ourselves, and living our own lives authentically is one of the best examples we can set for anyone. Figuring out what that means is worth the effort.

BIOGRAPHY

Kimberly O'Neill is your basic badass. She has magnetic enthusiasm and dynamic life experience with over twenty years in leadership development and lifestyle transitions. She has championed hundreds of workshops and coached thousands of people to face their fears, obliterate excuses, and level up to reach their goals. Kimberly served in the Air Force and government before transitioning to the network marketing industry, where she leads large teams and coaches individuals to succeed. Commitment to family and service to others led her to entrepreneurship as a speaker, author, and coach. She has inspired audiences from one to more than 2,000 and is known for her ability to motivate and drive people into action. Passionate about personal growth and mental toughness, Kimberly is highly credentialed and consistently pushes herself to new levels. She works from home in upstate NY, where she homeschools her children, maximizing all that life has to offer!

Connect with Kimberly O'Neill via https://linktr.ee/kimberlyoneill

CHAPTER 2

Journey To Success

By Matt Morris

As a speaker and coach for the past twenty years, I've been blessed to help several thousand people become full-time entrepreneurs with hundreds in the six-figure range and over fifty documented million-dollar earners.

It's also rewarded me with a lifestyle that I never would have imagined as a boy. If you would have told me I'd be a millionaire at twenty-nine, earn eight figures in my thirties and generate several billion in sales, all while adventuring to over eighty countries by my early forties; I wouldn't have believed you.

I also never imagined I'd be blessed with a career that fills me up with such immense levels of fulfillment and significance, knowing that I've been able to assist so many others in achieving what most would consider "boundless" levels of success.

The question I'm asked all the time is . . . How?

In asking that question, most people are looking for tactics and strategies. And I'll admit, early in my coaching days, I focused my mentorship almost solely on teaching the how-tos.

Unfortunately, that made me a pretty lousy coach.

I'd give them the tactics that allowed me to become a superstar salesperson, run a multi-million dollar company, or speak powerfully from stage.

My students would apply the how-tos and come back frustrated with mediocre improvements at best.

What I failed to realize in my early coaching days is a quote from the late Brian Klemmer that says, "If how-tos were enough, we'd all be rich, skinny, and happy."

As we explore the secrets to experiencing boundless levels of success, we must first examine what keeps us bound to our current situation.

Hint: It's NOT a lack of tactics and strategies.

With a quick google search, you can find hundreds of YouTube videos and blog posts that will teach you the strategies to having six-pack abs. The reason most don't have that six-pack isn't that they don't know the how-tos.

When it comes to making your goals a reality, whether that be to have a sexy body, to become a top sales leader in your company, to start your own business, or any other worthwhile dream, the ONLY thing holding you back from achieving that goal is your mental programming.

The challenge most face in achieving a grand visionary future for themselves is the fact that it runs so completely contrary to their current vision, or identity, that's running them now.

Your current identity is made up of the beliefs you currently hold to be true about yourself. It's essentially how you genuinely see yourself.

Your personal identity subconsciously influences every decision and action you make (or don't make), thus influencing the level of success you're able to achieve.

If your personal identity is that of someone who is out of shape or overweight, you may go on streaks where you eat right and exercise vigorously, but you tend to always shift right back into your old ways. Irresistible cravings, lethargy, sleeping in, etc., are somehow always overpowering your desire to be fit.

Why is that the case?

You'll want to write this down.

The Law of Commitment and Consistency

The law of commitment and consistency says that we will remain committed to remaining consistent with who we genuinely believe we are.

That being true, we must understand that in order to change our results, we have to change the beliefs we have about ourselves.

Let's take a deep dive into beliefs.

Take a look at the middle three letters of the word "beliefs," and what word do you see?

LIE

Consider for a moment that the story (the beliefs) you've been telling yourself about who you are as a person are simply lies you've made up.

Stories you may have accepted as "fact" like you're:

- Shy
- Self-conscious
- Lacking self-confidence
- Not a morning person
- Afraid of public speaking
- Not a good communicator
- Not as smart as the others

Would it be empowering to know that any of the negative beliefs above, along with countless others, are nothing more than lies you created subconsciously through a belief-building process you went through and didn't even know you were going through it?

What makes me so certain these "character traits" are lies? Because I had all of those beliefs about myself that I once accepted as fact.

Today, if you told me I was any of those things, I would laugh in your face because it would be completely absurd in my mind to accept any of those as true.

If you're willing to take a journey with me, I'll show you how I literally rewrote my entire identity from a broke, scarcity-filled, self-conscious young man into a confident and powerful multi-millionaire.

I'm here to tell you that whatever limiting beliefs you've created for yourself are absolute and total crap. I'm proof of it and many of those I've mentored for the past twenty years are proof of it.

I don't know what lies about yourself you've accepted as fact, but I know beyond a shadow of a doubt that, at your core, you are not a bad communicator, you are not unworthy of finding love, you are not a failure, you are not destined to always struggle, or any other negative belief.

Whatever they might be, you have the power to change those disempowering beliefs that serve only to limit the amount of success and personal fulfillment you experience.

If your current beliefs are what determine your success, the big question becomes how do you change your beliefs to create the results you want?

Before we answer that question, you first need to understand what shapes your beliefs in the first place. What has caused you to hold the beliefs that you do? Understanding where they came from will help you change them.

The belief building process you went through to come up with the beliefs you currently hold to be true have been shaped by three main factors:

1. Experiences
2. External programming
3. Internal programming

Experiences:

Every experience you've ever been through has been forever deposited and stored somewhere in your subconscious mind.

Maybe you were teased as a kid in school because you stuttered, and now you believe you're a poor communicator. Maybe you were laughed at in class as a kid for giving the wrong answer, and you took on a belief that you're not as smart as the other kids. Maybe you made a few horrible business choices when you were first starting out, and now you think you're lousy in business.

Whether you've realized it before now or not, those deposits were the first major factor that gave you the foundation of your identity.

Here's the way it works . . .

An event happens and then you make up a story (a belief) about what that event means.

Most of us tend to create a negative meaning based on what we perceive to be a negative experience. We create a victim story—I'm not loved because my parents abused me or left me. I'm a terrible business person because I failed for five years. People are not trustworthy because my business partner stole from me (all personal stories I made up at one point).

Think about some examples from your past. Can you think of some examples of events where you created a negative belief?

Real power comes from understanding that nothing has meaning until we give it meaning.

Events are neutral. It's the story we make up from the event that holds all the power. Rather than the victim story you may have been running in your mind, how can you create a new and empowering meaning based on that experience?

Understand—you have the power to choose. Victim or Victor. Which will it be?

External Programming:

Whether you want to believe this or not, you've been programmed.

Your parents programmed you as a child to believe certain things about yourself, other people, money, religion, and many other things.

The school system, your friends, the media, television, and other factors have programmed you to believe many of the things you do today.

Some of this programming has likely been healthy and gotten you to where you are and built you into the person you are today. Unfortunately, we also all have some less than empowering beliefs, and associated fears, that we've adopted as well from that external programming.

By the time you were two years old, you heard the word no thousands of times more than you heard the word yes. It's no wonder so many people, when presented with an opportunity to start a business or take on a challenge, are paralyzed with fear and are hesitant to take action.

At some point in your life, you've most likely faced a moment where someone said something negative to you or doubted your ability, without even meaning to. For a lot of people, that first comes from their parents and family members.

The things that people say to you, whether they intentionally mean harm or not, can profoundly shape who you are—*but only if you let it.* You obviously can't go back into the past and change the negative things you've heard, but you can make the decision right now to no longer let those things define you.

You can recognize that what someone says about you has no basis in reality unless you *choose* to believe it. It's a choice. A choice you can start making right now, today, to say **no more**.

Internal Programming:

More than your experiences and more than the voices of the people around you, the greatest and most powerful way your beliefs are shaped is from your internal programming. Thankfully, it's also the mechanism you have the most control over.

Every word that comes out of your mouth and every thought that comes out of your mind serves as a programming tool. Those thoughts and words get entered into your subconscious mind and then work to create your habitual routines and mental thought patterns.

Psychologists who study brain science agree that your subconscious mind is infinitely more powerful than your conscious mind. The subconscious is the driving force behind your belief system and your identity.

The subconscious mind has a goal that can serve you negatively or positively. That goal is to keep you in line with your identity. Remember the law of commitment and consistency?

If, based on your regular programming, you tell yourself you're broke, you're tired, and you suck as an entrepreneur, your subconscious mind figures out a way to keep you consistent with that programming.

If, however, you continually tell yourself you're wealthy, you're energized, and you're an amazing entrepreneur, your subconscious mind begins doing everything in its power to create *that* reality.

Here's the best way to understand it.

Whatever you say about yourself makes it more true.

If you say, *"I'm an idiot,"* you become more of an idiot. If you say, *"I'm a genius,"* you become more of a genius.

Your consistent programming creates your identity.

Here's the trick; your subconscious mind does not know the difference between the truth and a lie. It simply does its best to carry out exactly what you've programmed it to believe.

So when you say, "I'm sexy, I'm confident, I'm a millionaire," your conscious mind might be telling you you're full of it, but your subconscious mind, which is where the true power lies, will take that as a command and start working out a way for you to be all of those things.

The key to reprogramming your subconscious and changing your deep-seeded beliefs is to change your deposits. You do this by constantly filling your subconscious mind with empowering, uplifting, and motivating thoughts and words.

If you continually profess what you don't want, or focus on the things you don't have or aren't, then you actually attract more of that negativity and continue to reinforce more of that personal identity. **What you focus on expands.**

BIOGRAPHY

Author of the international bestseller, *The Unemployed Millionaire*, Matt Morris began his career as a serial entrepreneur aged eighteen. Since then, he has generated over $1.5 billion through his sales organizations, with a total of over one million customers worldwide. As a self-made millionaire and one of the top internet and network marketing experts, he's been featured on international radio and television and spoken from platforms to audiences in over twenty-five countries around the world. And now, as the founder of Success Publishing, he co-authors with leading experts from every walk of life.

Contact Matt Morris via http://www.MattMorris.com

CHAPTER 3

The Person You Could Have Been

By Steve Moreland

If Fate's blood-stained cauldron has not found your life yet, she's hiding just over the horizon, waiting until you're at your most vulnerable. So if you're willing to listen to someone that knows about life's ash heap, I'll share the Lessons I learned *after* I failed my Test. The lessons focus on our thinking. More specifically, about how thinking differently empowered me to *thrive* where most cannot imagine surviving. I promise not to waste your time with fluffy bullshit or rah-rah! Just the mental tools what worked, that brought me across a desert wilderness of 5,544 days.

May the following battle-tested advice return you from your seemingly impossible cauldron *"tested—and found not wanting."*

We Texans pride ourselves on our Code. Toughness is Rule #1. And it means *"no tears allowed."* See, our cult-like indoctrination begins the moment we are born. And the other Spartan rules include: *do only BIG things*, especially if others say it can't be done; *rub some dirt on it* because blood and scars prove your worth; and *do Right*, even if the Lord God, himself, threatens you to do otherwise!

Brutal. Absolutely! But definitely the kind of folks you'd want covering your back in a fight. It's a belief carved deep in our soul—that there simply is NO FREE LUNCH. It is a creed rooted in commitment and perseverance, summed up in one word. Grit!

The standard we have to carry begins early. At age twelve, I started *"earning my worth."* My phone rang off the wall with grass- cutting jobs in the Texas infernos called summer because my dad drilled me to do what everyone else is afraid of, to deliver results beyond expectations. Just self-disciplined results! No excuses.

I went right to corporate America after graduating with academic scholarships – working for three Fortune 500 companies before I was 24. At twenty-five I was in charge of my own brokerage firm in Dallas. By thirty, I'd made it to millionaire status, flew in private jets, brokered 9-figure deals from European castles, banked in numbered Swiss accounts, and spoke on international stages raising millions for venture capital deals.

Ballistic was my term for the vertical climb I experienced. Simultaneously serving as vice president of offshore operations for a boutique hedge fund, CEO of a 58-office tax and wealth management firm, and co-principal of a SaaS startup. I couldn't afford the luxury of sleep. And part of every month, I lived near my office in the banking district of Nassau, Bahamas, acting as the vice president of business development for a middle eastern banking syndicate.

Occasionally, I woke up at a place my then-wife and children called home. It was there that I slowed down enough to rub some of that Texas dirt on my hand tremors from sleeping only on those overseas flights. I was stumbling forward just to maintain the pace. There was something wrong but I could not risk failing the mission. My Dad's standing orders were crystal: *"You can rest when you're dead!"* And this belief came from his creed that a man only earns a medal on his gravestone if he dies "in combat."

Well, I failed to become a "lifer" in the Corps, so I determined that I was going to achieve whatever most would call impossible. I believed in his invincibility! And after eighteen years of his Marine- style bootcamp, I feared only one thing, **"meeting the person I could have been!"**

So, when Fate's blood-stained hurricane came for me, I was Ready. Ready to blindly march into Hell itself. But after the first few years, I felt more like the Greek myth of Sisyphus who was sentenced to pushing a boulder up the mountain every damn day and then waking up the next morning to find it at the bottom again. I remember thinking to myself, "Maybe God is *not* good" after feeling soul-crushing agony for the first time. Real pain that made me wish I could just die and get it over.

I'll admit, all that invincibility crap did NOT work. And I'm painfully embarrassed to admit that I found myself wallowing in my self-pity after losing absolutely everything and feeling abandonment by all I loved. I had succumbed to that state of a *victim*. And you know what, that Texas dirt did NOT fix the wounds I'd caused my family for the undeserved trials and tribulations my bull-headed foolishness caused.

Though I was brought up with my dad's relentless Texan and Marine Corp code of conduct mixed with my mom's Christian beliefs, the devasting pain caused me to question their beliefs. Sitting in the ash heap of my life like the Bible's character Job, I commenced to blaming God for not protecting us from the horror that imprisoned us. I begged and even prayed for an instant release of misery, even raising my fist in anger and shouting "You're *NOT* a good god!"

I just wanted that magical snap of a finger and everything to be like it used to be. But genie-like fixes never happen, do they. Why? Because strength is *not* forged in luxury and comfort. Medals do not get pinned to your chest for holding hands and singing "Kum Ba Yah."

The struggle to endure real agony, to eat suffering, and know your pain so intimately that you name her has a purpose. You see, it took time for me to get over my self-entitlement in order to face my demons and do the most excruciating thing I'd ever done. Realizing that I could not change the past or erase what my mistakes had cost my family, I had to make a decision: either continue to blame others and wallow in self-pity or use the hell I was inside to forge a better version of me!

In school, we're first taught the lesson that prepares us for the test. But, in life, we face the Test first; later, we learn the Lesson.

The grade is what we become through it all. It's pass or fail. And yes, hell is when you meet that person you could have been. It means rising again and again within the blood-stained cauldron of Fate. Only this repeated discipline distinguishes the few from the many, the extraordinary from the ordinary. The worthy from the worthless.

But that person you could have been is only Hell if he or she stands better than you chose to become! **Hell, then, is meeting the *better* person you could have been.**

Like I promised in the beginning, what follows WILL take you through any hell. And you will arrive on the other side, *"tested – and found not wanting."*

Let's begin with a question: "Have you ever been really curious about something—to the point of obsession?"

Since I was a kid, I wanted to unravel this thing called thinking. I reasoned to myself that if I could only understand how the few we call "great" actually thought, I might be able to be like them and make the world a little bit better. Because, for the most part, they are human just like me. The only difference is that they *see things differently* in their minds.

Personal development "coaches" blather about managing our thinking. It is THE key, agreed. But it's not enough to know *what* to do. We've got to know *how* to do it. It's the subtle and often <u>hidden difference</u> <u>between learning science without the art of knowing how it applies to</u> <u>real-world situations</u>. Most of these "well-meaning" coaches deserve an "A" for science but an

"F" in art. Never earning a medal from within Fate's blood-stained cauldron means their theories can get you to one destination – that chance to meet the person you could have been.

Here's an example of a coach with earned rank, Dr. Viktor Frankl – author of *Man's Search For Meaning*. Frankl didn't just survive six years of Nazi concentration camps, he changed the world forever with his discovery of how we create meaning through our imagination.

Better thinking creates better doing. And better doing creates a better being.

Frankl forced me to think. I mean really think. And all of a sudden, what Professor Eli Goldratt wrote in *The Goal* became crystal clear. "If we continue to do what we have done, which is what everybody else is doing, we will continue to get the same *unsatisfactory* result." But I asked myself, isn't that what we do so very often - more of what everyone else has done and then expecting a different outcome?

We are what we've done, right? So, aren't our own actions - what we *do* - that creates who we *become*? In short, "doing creates being." So, who we are today – our being, is a product of our past doings? Becoming someone better can only happen by doing differently. And differently results from the seed of the thoughts in our imagination.

Because I wanted a different future – one that honored the sacred by making the world better, I could no longer afford to think like I used to, or like everyone else. Maybe you're brighter than me and already know this. But for me, this realization was the Eureka! And in that realization, I felt something deep inside like lightning.

If my prior thinking caused my current doings (my actions and habits that are known as my reality), **then why couldn't I change my future by changing the way I was thinking?**

Socrates (Greek philosopher 470 B.C.) taught a Secret passed through his student Plato to his student Aristotle (Greek philosopher 384 B.C.). Aristotle planted this Secret into the mind of a 13-year-old prince. This Secret method of thinking changed the ancient world.

At 16 years of age, the prince led his cavalry at the Battle of Chaeronea, decimating a supposedly unbeatable enemy. At 20 years of age, he became king of Greece, marched his army towards Persia, solved the riddle of the Gordian Knot, and destroyed any that opposed.

At 24, he captured the supposedly unconquerable city of Tyre. At 25, he became Pharaoh of Egypt and then returned to the desert near modern-day Babylon to lead his 50,000-man army against a force exceeding 500,000 led by the Persian emperor Darius. Charging into the front line on his legendary black stallion Bucephalus, he achieved the impossible and became emperor of the known world.

By age 30, he had created the largest empire in history. Today, he's still studied in war colleges for his battlefield genius, ethical governance, and unrivaled valor.

The Secret thought? "Be as you wish to seem."

The Result? One *impossible* difficulty after another - CRUSHED!

His Name? Alexander

How is he remembered? Alexander—the Great!

In school, we're first taught the lesson that prepares us for the test. But, in life, we face the Test first; later, we learn the Lesson.

Here's my experience. The Lessons learned *after* the Test lead to better actions—which lead to becoming a better being, right? That means that tests uncover our weaknesses so that we can learn greater lessons. What and who we become through the Tests reflects our grade in life.

If we're honest, we'll admit that we often create our own storms. And then we blame others when we must endure them. But if we use the agony, we find something called grit. Grit is commitment bathed in love to become better than we were the day before. It's a relentless dedication to rise—to become better, stronger, and wiser. It's a refusal to quit, even when we feel we can't get up again.

The question is, will we? Will we persist after the problems that were caused by our poor thinking – and the results that followed? Or will we just quit due to the fear of failing and the probability that life won't be easy?

Being *"tested and found not wanting"* means we'll certainly be scarred from one battle after another. But the scars reflect rank, defining how many times we returned to the cauldron instead of hiding and waiting to be rescued by the God that's testing us.

It may be cliché, but our very thinking sparks our every action. Put another way, our doings, added together over time, construct our being - *what* and *who* we become.

Do we dishonor the Sacred, settling for what everybody else is doing and continuing to get their same *unsatisfactory* results?

Or do we *think* **better**, in order to *do* **better**, so that we could *be* **better?**

We become what we choose to be. This is the Secret. My gift to you, as Aristotle long ago shared with Alexander, "be[come] as you wish to seem."

Now you know that Hell is NOT meeting the person you could have been.

Hell is meeting the *better* person you could have been.

BIOGRAPHY

A native Texan, Steve Moreland is known for two things. Dedicated practice. And success. Success equates to one's level of practice. So he really does only one thing. His Rubicon system teaches how to perform the common under uncommon conditions. Motivated by the Latin creed FORTES FORTUNA ADIUVAT – "Fortune favors the brave," his mission is to deliberately cause affirmative outcomes that would not have occurred otherwise.

Connect with Steve via https://linktr.ee/steve_moreland

CHAPTER 4

Shaky Beginnings

By Adrien Fouillard

I am just an ordinary guy. It took me fifty-three years to realize that ordinary was not going to get me ahead. I was really just a quintessential follower and people pleaser. Building a successful life was not that important to me. Pleasure-seeking and recreational activities took firm precedence.

I was fortunate to have been raised in a great family by loving parents and siblings. My parents both served people on a daily basis. They truly took their eyes off themselves and put them on others. They were the best role models ever! I am proud to share that my father was a World War II veteran, having served in the Air Force throughout the war. It was always in my subconscious to join the Canadian Forces.

At fourteen, my parents sent me 200 miles away to a Catholic school, where I boarded at a seminary. This was in hopes of getting at least one priest out of eight boys. I resented their decision and rebelled. During this period, a couple of disgraceful incidents took place: nearly overdosing on LSD and eventually getting kicked out of the seminary, just so my parents could find me a new home. Schooling was easy for me, so I was still able to graduate four years later despite all my immaturity. A couple of hurtful events followed in the next few years: one of these was the loss of a nephew and niece, whose lives were taken by cystic fibrosis at the very young age of eight. I just did not find that fair and needed to lean into my faith through those great losses.

One would think that I learned my lesson, but through the years, the pleasure-seeking, destructive patterns continued through college and various jobs. One shattering experience with an unwanted pregnancy between two irresponsible kids (my girlfriend and me) made me rethink my position in life. It was a tough lesson, but we mutually ended the relationship through decisions out of our control. I now needed to figure out my next step in life. As I reflected on my past lesson, I decided to make a second attempt to join the Canadian Navy at the age of twenty-three in 1991. My application to the Airforce in 1986, at eighteen, was rejected because of the drugs in my system at the time (a very embarrassing situation). However, this time was different; I was recruited in the Navy as a Naval Weapons Technician.

I am proud to say that I made it through basic training, winning the Platoon Achievement Award (an award for someone who sucks at everything, but I never gave up and figured it out). In the first year, en route to Halifax, while on party mode during graduation night, I was charged for driving under the influence. I lost my license for a year. As I mentioned, on my first deployment, I was fortunate to participate in a six-month peacekeeping mission in 1992. This took place in the Persian Gulf, aboard the HMCS Restigouche. I got to see a bit of the world during this voyage, being initiated from Tadpole to Shellback by crossing the Equator and crossing the International Date Line. This meant that I had started my voyage on the West Coast and completed it after a full tour around the world and ending up on the West Coast. Pretty cool!

The most important part, and the greatest thing ever about my joining the Navy, was that after this six-month voyage, at the end of September (on the 29th, to be precise), I met Stacey: the beautiful and smart woman who I would soon call my wife! Things moved pretty quickly with us. At first, I moved in with her as just a roommate. But this lasted about a week after the two of us developed feelings beyond just being roommates—if you know what I mean. This escalated, and the two of us were married on May 01, 1993, and Stacey gave birth to Christian on December 24, 1993.

Side note. If you do the math, she was already pregnant before we were married—something my mother eventually figured out.

Life started great! I loved sailing and learning the trade, but I was missing valuable time with my family. Instead, I just numbed myself with alcohol to mask the sadness. I would call my wife when I was in foreign ports, wishing the family could be with me. However, a lack of money did not allow that. As difficult as it was, I signed a second contract. I was offered a move to Halifax with my family to attend a two-year Naval Weapons Technician course at the engineering school in Stadacona.

Gratitude was not in my dictionary—not until after this scary situation! Our second son, Nathaniel, was born three and a half weeks premature due to complications with placenta abruption. Luckily, both survived, just short of fifteen minutes! It was crazy how it worked out! I am not proud to say this, but I was about a half-hour away, inebriated after having helped a friend move into a new house. When Stacey called me, I knew something was majorly wrong; she could not move off the couch and was in pain. I phoned Grace Hospital, and they informed me to get her there as quickly as I could, as they would not be able to get to her quickly enough. Just the thought of losing her and my son instantly sobered me. That is my story. It was a blur! This story is a true success, even with my poor decision of drinking and driving once again. But this time, it was for a much better reason. I got her to the hospital, with her feeling every bump and me racing through red lights and rushing through traffic. Luckily, it was evening, and traffic was pretty mild. Great turnout! The emergency was a success: mom and baby were safe. However, Nathaniel was hospitalized in an incubator for a week. Today, he is a very healthy twenty-six-year-old. As I alluded to earlier, that was truly my first real lesson about gratitude. Through these challenging situations, my faith gave me strength.

I was in fleet school, and my wife and kids were homed in military housing. We were hardly making ends meet. At times, we had to sneak some money out of the kids' piggy bank to purchase a jug of milk—a pretty sad situation, I know. We eventually figured out how to tighten our budget, and at times, we were blessed with grandma sending us care packages and treats. Sometimes, she would even slip in a fifty-dollar bill. Things always seemed to work out.

After my course graduation in Halifax, we moved back to Victoria, where I sailed for another year and a half. Because of much time at sea and not being able to prioritize time with family, both Stacey and I agreed that I would end my second naval contract in 1997 and pursue a career in hydraulics, which led us to Manitoba. Trying to impress my employer and coworkers, I embarked on a workaholic, overtime-filled journey, almost forgetting I had a wife and two kids at home. Occasionally, I would use my hard work as an excuse to go drinking. What a jerk I can be at times!

While we were in Winnipeg, I experienced the most humbling, enriching, and probably one of my saddest moments ever: the passing of my sister, Sarah. She passed away at the age of forty-one, taken by cancer while pregnant, losing her baby in the process. She was also the mother of the two children who passed away from cystic fibrosis years earlier. Sarah left behind her husband and four children. The humbling part of this story was that I got to spend a few hours each weeknight with Sarah and got to know the amazing heart she had for people and the joy she spread with her servant heart, beautiful smile, and courage, despite her difficult life. Sarah was truly loved by all who were blessed to cross her path. The children's hospital staff even held a memorial for her; her many years of service there had an impact on them. I would go to the hospital from work, tired from the day, and five minutes after being around her made me forget all about my woes and made me look at life with positivity and a smile. She had that impact on people. It was a huge lesson in attitude from the greatest teacher ever!

The next phase of life brought our family to Alberta, two provinces away, where we reside today. Stacey was hired by my brother and his new drilling company, and I pursued my career in hydraulics. Still engulfed in my bad habits of overworking and alcohol, my home life began to suffer. In 2003, Stacey and I started our own hydraulic business, building a good reputation in that industry. In the same year, our third son, Noah, was born. The destructive patterns continued, and as a result of our caustic home situation, a member of my family was negatively impacted, and I was nearly too late to respond. But my faith came through for my family, and the situation eventually was mended. The acreage life was great for a while, but the endless maintenance while still running a business had finally taken its toll. We suffered through the 2008–2010 recession, made it through, and before rehiring manpower again, decided to sell our assets, clear our debt, and work for the man again. I feel that if I had decided to continue without Stacey, we would not be together today. That was probably the best decision I ever made! I'm a slow learner, but I'm still learning.

In 2010, around the same time, my sister Rosalie passed away at the age of fifty-three due to esophageal cancer. She left a husband and seven children behind—another tough blow, especially for her family. She, also like Sarah, was an impactful leader in the community and was loved by everyone.

With the pressure of running a business removed for the next few years, things progressed as normal as we could hope. I was genuinely making an effort to be there for my family more and taking up some small hobbies such as minor gunsmithing (I even took an online course and got the certificate). The routine thing on a Saturday was to enjoy a few drinks and play in the garage with my lathe and guns. It was fun and relaxing, but I knew deep down there had to be something more. There were parts of me that still missed the hustle and bustle of my own business.

A couple of other challenging moments in my life that I would need another chapter just to elaborate on are the instant passing of my father in 2004 (he died of a severe heart attack) and the death of my mother in 2016, after five years of suffering from a stroke. Through those most brutal years of her life, I believe she positively impacted people's lives through her fight and determination.

In 2016, my life journey took a path for the better. Educating myself from books and personal mentors had me learning lessons long overdue. A few of these are the importance of family, empathy for others, and letting go of the status quo. Finally, getting my drinking under control, learning how to let status and ego not control my life, and not worrying about what people think of me are a few more things I have been working on. The list of what I learn every day keeps building up, which leads me to share my story.

BIOGRAPHY

Adrien Fouillard has had experience in various fields of business. Some of the positions he held are a sailor in the Canadian Navy, small business owner, service manager, successful entrepreneur, and network marketer. He has sailed around the world, moved his family from coast to coast, and experienced life to the fullest along his journey. His educational achievements and accreditations include Naval Weapons Technician, Certified Fluid Power Hydraulic Specialist, Certified Engineering Technician, and Gunsmith. Adrien's proudest accomplishments are husband and father. Through many life lessons and mentorship, Adrien has been able to put things behind him that were holding him back from achieving a great life. He now believes that sharing some of those lessons could be instrumental in creating significance for others. Adrien has been married to Stacey since 1993, and they have three boys: Christian, Nathaniel, and Noah.

Connect with Adrien Fouillard via https://linktr.ee/Sailor67

CHAPTER 5

Reboot Your Mindset

By Anastacia Njoroge

Six in the morning—it was time to wake up! The familiar song *Amka Kumekucha*, meaning, 'Wake up its dawn!' in Swahili, played on the radio. The song went on to say: 'It's time to go to school. Education is the key to building a nation . . .' These memories make their way into my mind quite often. The programming started at a very early age.

7:15 am was a crucial hour! If you were not ready, my dad, who was waiting outside with his Volkswagen Beetle, would rather you find your own way to school! It was on these school rides that my dad would pour out his one-liner: 'You see, child, the CEOs and the rich are the ones driving the BMWs and on the road at 6 am.' Without a mention, you'd hear it clearly: 'Child, I want you to be like that CEO.' This child wanted to be that person. My mind was set!

Jim Rohn says that we are the average of the five people we spend the most time with.[1] To achieve anything, you will need to surround yourself with the people who have been successful in the very thing you desire. I did not know this truth then, but I was engaged in the earnest

---

1   Aimee Groth, "You're The Average Of The Five People You Spend The Most Time With," Business Insider (Business Insider, July 24, 2012), https://www. businessinsider.com/jim-rohn-youre-the-average-of-the-five-people-you-spend-the-most-time-with-2012-7?IR=T.

pursuit of becoming that CEO with a BMW who wakes up very early in the morning!

My parents, siblings, and their friends were my mentors. I listened to them when they told me education was key, and CEOs had MBAs. Taking their words to heart, I enrolled myself in a college in Kenya which taught business studies. The journey had begun!

During this time, I heard that CEOs who were doing well obtained their degrees from abroad. Craving the same success, I knew I had to grab the opportunity to shine with a degree from a well-known institute in the USA or the UK. This would definitely be the key to my CEO status!

I landed in the UK on a cold autumn day. I was a big girl, with big dreams, in a big world! I knew no one here! I loved the friends I made, and I loved the university I attended. I performed well in my academics, and like any teen, I had my fun with parties and clubbing. Fast forward, and I earned my degree. I was ready to become a CEO!

Life hit me hard when I began applying for jobs. I faced rejection after rejection. So, I settled for an odd job just to keep up with the bills.

Remember the Swahili song that played at 6 am? Education is key? I thought perhaps I needed to top up my degree, and then I would find a good job! Once again, I found myself enrolling for a master's degree with the strong, unshakable hope that I would land a decent job that would help me climb the corporate ladder to CEO status. But life hit hard— again—with endless job applications coming back as endless rejections!

My mind started telling me things—things that would justify why I was unable to get a job. Maybe because I was a foreigner? Perhaps because I lacked CV writing skills? Was it the colour of my skin? My last name? When you really need to know the answer, your mind will dig deep and find something—some meaning—for you to latch on to.

I finally reached a point where I heard enough! I pictured going back to those six-am-mornings and smashing that radio on the floor. I was done with education! PhD? What is that? I was done! I was ready to take hold of my life and lead it *my* way. I can resonate with anyone who quits school to pursue their interests, because that was what I did.

I worked for a few years to pay my bills, but the job market was uncertain. Some months were good, and some were not. The struggle was real. I experienced back-breaking work only to be broke. I recall calling up my father and telling him how broke I was. His reply was simple: 'You can be broke. But don't be broken!' That statement really did something for me. It felt like a call from my ancestors. It woke up my warrior spirit—the spirit that says, "Don't give up!" Enough of living paycheck to paycheck! I knew there was a better way, and that life had something much better in store than what I had then. Yet, figuring it out was a massive puzzle. I had all the pieces, but they were just not adding up, which drove me nuts. But I was determined to piece them together.

I was now back in my home country, Kenya. Back home, there is an unwritten rule that whoever lived and worked abroad had to be rich. When abroad, we take photos of the beautiful sceneries and well-paved roads. Our skin looks better and brighter because the weather is more favourable to it. The movies and TV shows help spread the lie very well that everyone from western countries is rich. When we travel back home, after saving for months, we buy nice clothing apparel and sport an acquired accent. We become all the envy. Because of this, most of the locals wish to go to the land of milk and honey.

The last time was in my home country, I witnessed something that I had never seen before. People around me were doing significantly better than I was. My peers had moved on and did well for themselves, living in much better houses than I did here in the UK. Seeing this, the heavens opened, and rays of light shone upon me. It was a lightbulb moment, or rather, a for-heaven's-sake moment.

I realized that the Land of Milk and Honey was everywhere! I've had talks with friends who shared their frustrations. They were told to study, work hard, and pursue higher education; the reward would be a good job. The reality was that this was a myth for many. The majority of those who were brainwashed by this succumbed to frustrations and lived in dire stress and poor conditions. Not knowing where else to look, they felt disappointed and betrayed because of their inability to seek a better future.

Following my heaven's sake moment, I returned to England with new eyes, a new attitude, and a renewed spirit. It was then when I began to question everything I had previously been taught. Religion, education, wealth, and money. Information on all of these is out there, but one has to sift through all the propaganda. I reflected on the past, and I felt betrayed by the very same people I had looked up to, believed, and worshiped. I went through all five stages of grief. First, you go through denial: how can you differentiate between the truth and lies? Then, you become angry with yourself. It's not until you accept the reality of what happened that you can finally move on.

I was now enrolled in the School of Life. In this school, I found my mentors, guides, and teachers for life. They came in and went out depending on the stage of learning in which I found myself.

My biggest takeaway (and I invite you to take this with you) was this: Mindset is Everything!

You only have *one* mind, and it was shaped long before you could say 'dada.' The environment in which you grew up, your guardians, and everyone around whom you grew up has helped shape and form your beliefs, values, and attitude. This is the mind you have, and you carry it with you wherever you go. And everywhere you go, you will find yourself in the same situation time and again. In the words of Albert Einstein: "We cannot solve our problems with the same thinking we used when we created them."[2] Ding!!

Our culture has drilled into our minds the belief that education is the key. In my pursuit of 'CEO status,' I firmly held on to that belief. But I kept finding myself stuck between the proverbial rock and hard place every single time. Insanity. My friend, Einstein, also said, "The definition of insanity is doing the same thing over and over again, but expecting

---

2   "Albert Einstein Quotes," BrainyQuote (Xplore), accessed June 22, 2021, https://www.brainyquote.com/quotes/albert_einstein_121993.

different results."[3] I had to prepare myself for the same results unless I changed my mode of thinking. In other words: my mindset needed a reboot.

Be ready to challenge the status quo and confront everything you believe to be true. Perform a total mind recall and inquire as to whether your beliefs serve you or not. I found many of my beliefs to be wanting. I had to think in an entirely different manner if I wanted to pursue my— say it with me—CEO status.

I learned that if I wanted to become the other person (in this case, a CEO), I had to study that person. I had to identify who that was, look up to them, and emulate them. So, I made it my mission to study success.

I started with the Bible and found several references to a God who wanted us to prosper and be in good health, who wanted to show us the land of milk and honey. On the contrary, religion taught me that I needed to sacrifice, and that God was a God of punishment. All of it was contrary to what I read. I delved into studying other religions and found the same thing. I love the Bible, so I know what truths to hold to, and I cling on to them like a leech. You cannot change one's ideology, but you must pursue the truth for your own sake. Then, I began studying successful people. Instead of watching TV series, I would watch interviews of the world's successful people, a practice I follow to date.

Unfortunately, the mind wants what is comfortable and familiar, so it will try to trick you. This will feel like going against a tornado. Any new information, your mind will resist with the following thought: 'They became successful because they had all the resources to do so. They are successful because *insert reason*.' Ignore such thoughts and keep moving forward. Immerse yourself entirely in unlearning and learn new ways of thinking and new ways of being. Do this until you become the person you desire to be.

---

3   Trent Hamm, "If You Want Different Results, You Have to Try Different Approaches," The Simple Dollar, November 11, 2020, https://www. thesimpledollar.com/make-money/if-you-want-different-results-you-have-to-try-different-approaches/.

Remember that apart from TV, we also have books. I was an avid reader of novels. I have missed one too many stops, having been engrossed in murder mystery novels. Since then, I have swapped this genre for autobiographies, how-to books, and new skills.

Acquiring skills was something that was never taught to me growing up. The only skills we were encouraged to pursue were those of being a doctor, lawyer, engineer, and maybe an accountant. Those were the only skills worth pursuing, and woe to you if your grades did not meet the standards because that deemed your future gloomy.

Oh! How I *do not* miss the days when you'd get the stick for getting a low grade. This indirectly taught us that failure was bad. Sadly, this is a struggle for many who are in pursuit of success. The very thought of failing is so paralysing that they would rather not pursue success. I've been there. You just have to really press on!

There are plenty of opportunities out there, my friends. If only you would open your mind to all the possibilities. Do not let your childhood programming keep you down. Forgive the past and look forward to a brighter future.

The world is in a constant state of flux, and we have to change with it. Case in point, the COVID-19 pandemic. It caught many people off-guard. But those who were prepared with their bank accounts did not feel the effects.

Futureproof yourself today, press the reset button, and reboot your mindset! I challenge you to learn a new skill, learn where the market is going, and learn the skills needed to stay on par with the market. Then, go find a mentor, a course, and a book that will teach you the skill. *This* is how you prepare for opportunities that will come knocking at the door.

Now, you may have a burning question: Did I achieve my CEO status?

Well, my friends. Yes, I did. I am the CEO of my life, and I want you to be the CEO of your life as well. Take control, be the driver, change your mindset, and watch your life change!

BIOGRAPHY

Anastacia Njoroge is an MBA Graduate who grew up in Nairobi, Kenya. A self-made entrepreneur with a passion for personal development, she believes that it all begins with the mind, and there are no limitations to the mind except those we accept. She believes that it is never too late for one to reboot their mind and transform their life. The Bible is one of her instructors. She lives by the motto: "Do not conform to the pattern of this world, but be transformed by the renewing of your mind" (Romans 12:2 NIV).

Connect with Anastacia Njoroge at https://linktr.ee/AnastaciaN

CHAPTER 6

To Be A Living Student

By Asmait Yohannes

The success of an entrepreneurial venture lies in learning. An entrepreneur who has knocked on the doors of success is not only good at *how* to learn but also the mechanics of *what* to learn. They eventually organize their entire schedule of learning in alignment with their work/life. Millions of books and articles explain the same old beliefs of what it takes to stand out as a successful entrepreneur. The composition or traits usually involve the topics of excellent teams, luck, timing, imagination, passion, hard work, attractive market opportunities, innovative products, and great teams. Although all of the above-mentioned aspects are true, the essence of a successful business today is *Change*. The only constants in today's business are *Evolution* and *Change*. If one is to keep up with it, constant learning is a necessity.

A culture of constant learning is vital to an entrepreneur who strives to stand out in the realm of innovation and improvement. The foundation for all new ideas is knowledge and the commitment to constant learning. These enhance the malleability of the brain to form disruptive and innovative solutions.

Business in today's century moves at a breakneck pace as compared to twenty years ago. Accordingly, entrepreneurs are supposed to pivot, adapt, and grow into the spaces created in the market if they wish to survive. But if one is to talk about growth and expansion, then a team is always required to enhance an entrepreneur's vision. And the team solely depends on the leadership skills of the successful entrepreneur. An entrepreneur's success relies solely on continuously learning all kinds of skills—technical skills and soft skills like negotiating, interpersonal skills, and adaptability.

Being a life-long student tends to come in different forms. There are numerous ways to do so, but this chapter will highlight six of them.

#1 Book Reading

Book reading is an art that is lost in many nations. It could be a differentiating factor for a successful entrepreneur.

#2 Podcast Learning

There are numerous podcasts available online. For instance, TED talks have abundantly inspiring and informative podcasts. An entrepreneur will become successful through the leadership skills and tips taught in these podcasts.

#3 Conferences, Keynotes, and Seminars

There are numerous industry trends that one needs to be in pace with so as to grow their network and enhance their skills.

#4 Mentorship

If the living student is to be given a formal label, it is 'Student of a Mentor.' Most successful entrepreneurs and leaders believe in the process of mentorship. Their mentors often challenge the comfort bubble in which a person lives. They give an entrepreneur the added courage to step in and take risks.

#5 Networking

A living student needs to meet new people who can present them multiple learning opportunities. A living student works best when learning is all-rounded and holistic. Entrepreneurship can either be a dance or a walk on a tightrope depending on how focused or prepared a person is. Continuous learning and being a living student tend to be the catalysts that speed up the journey to success, helping empower and create a sense of balance and growth.

#6 Digitalization: Who Learns, Wins!

Every other company feels the need to train their employees further to keep up with the latest developments. This will also promote their own careers.

If you rest, you rust—this proverb holds much truth, shown through digitalization among entrepreneurs. If that code of conduct numbs your mind, you lose the ability to think beyond it. Don't get me wrong. Abiding by a set of values is great but abiding by a set of tried and tested patterns is debilitating to your personal development and to those of everyone associated with your company.

Digitization affects all levels of the hierarchy. HR managers would agree that technology has strongly changed and progressed everyday work in their companies. It doesn't matter if you have a small-sized company, a medium one, or a giant conglomerate, you will find repercussions of technological advancement in your company. And mind you, it's not just the IT department that takes the heat; the effects are far-reaching. You will find the company's middle management executives, trained specialists, clerks, and top executives to be under the influence of technological incognizance.

Whoever Learns, Wins

There are a lot of courses on "How to Become an Entrepreneur." And while you can learn about the technicalities and conduct of it all, these courses cannot teach you to be adaptable. However, you can learn how to use new communication tools and digital applications. Whoever learns, wins, and they have a better chance of gaining bigger career opportunities, more responsibility, or a raise in salary.

However, there is no point in simply taking any course by chance. Does the company need technicians, master craftsmen, or specialists with appropriate advancement training, for example? Or does further training in innovation management or project management lead to the goal?

These are the three most important employee competencies in the digitized work world:

1. Willingness to Learn
2. Flexibility
3. IT Know-How

Deciphering the Secret of Economic Success

The perfection of a creative mind lies in its ability to learn. Learning is the only pathway to success, whatever the task you choose for yourself. In this section, we will attempt to decipher the secret of entrepreneurial success.

Now you may ask, are successful entrepreneurs actually more capable of learning than other people?

A definite and resounding *YES*. They have to be. If they don't learn, they will perish. In modern markets, entrepreneurs have to constantly change their products and technologies. They have to learn what customers and their bankers want. That contextual knowledge will set their business apart and give them the edge to sell when customers look at their offerings.

One thing that adds value to a learning mindset is its ability to change. Many successful people have a firm grasp of when and how to change as per the challenge or situation that presents itself. Learning also creates a system of self-development on different levels. You can start at a simple level and then keep moving up. The capitalist dynamic requires people to climb higher levels. It is neither enough to absorb knowledge nor is it enough to learn how to learn. You have to acquire entrepreneurial energy to face challenges. You cannot cope with the pressure of problems if you do not acquire methods of extracting such energies from nothing, so to speak.

Now, there is a difference between the development and learning levels derived from them. These four learning levels are structured hierarchically. An entrepreneur is on the *routine* level in day-to-day business, i.e., the lowest. If he speculates on the stock market, buys other companies, or looks for cheaper labour, he has reached the level of *arbitrageur*. If he tries new things, he is an *innovator*. And if he develops himself, he is an *evolutionary entrepreneur*—this is the highest level.

The four functions correspond to four learning levels. If the entrepreneur does not learn anything, the routine remains intact. But when he introduces a new accounting system or learns how to address new customers, i.e., how to improve his communication skills, he is at a higher level of learning. The highest level would be when he learns how to change his previous routine with meaning. Whoever manages to do that is no longer a routine entrepreneur. The predominant type of economic man in Western teaching—who only reproduces what has been learned once—remains at the basic level. For an innovative entrepreneur, on the other hand, daily learning is essential. This also includes communicative and emotional skills. Without them, even good products can hardly be placed in the market. Those who cannot communicate properly cannot breathe success.

The highest level of learning is also the level of self-evolution. What distinguishes an entrepreneur at the highest level of learning is the degree of reflection on the levels below. For example, he might think, 'Why am I having problems with my banker? The business plan is correct; all the other data is also correct.' He has to be able to see why he is not getting along emotionally with the banker. Let's say maybe because he wasn't sensitive enough or didn't speak his language. So, he has to observe himself in order to recognize his own deficits.

For an entrepreneur, there is a way to get to the highest level. Which philosophical or spiritual school he entrusts himself to is his business. Successful entrepreneurs often have a strong spiritual component. They combine strong goals with great humility and reflection. And they have learned to quench negative emotions like fear or envy because these emotions negatively impact interaction with others.

Are Emotions a Secret to Business Success?

An innovative entrepreneur does things that he cannot calculate beforehand. Therefore, his character needs a strong emotional, intuitive, and creative element. The more radical the innovation, the more he has to get involved with this element.

In the western economy, emotions have a downright negative connotation. But Homo economicus, the calculator who runs a program in his head, does not work in the innovative field. A different kind of rationality is required for this.

Anyone who wants to address customers with a new product needs emotional competence for an unpredictable world. He needs empathy, i.e., the ability to empathize with other people. This is necessary for an innovator. He has to get into other people's psyche as market research data is not enough.

There are critics who could counter the decline of the new economy: too much imagination, too much emotionality, too little factual orientation. There is a vast body of research showing that many failed start-ups were run by emotionally weak people. They had difficulty getting out of their software logic and understanding what needs their customers really have. On the other hand, those who remained successful, such as eBay or Amazon, had a high level of emotional and communicative competence at the management level.

They were able to differentiate between acquiring fertile knowledge and sluggish knowledge. There was too much sluggishness. Fertile knowledge is put into action. Idle knowledge is only carried around in the head.

Vision is a very popular term. A vision has many components and is very comprehensive. The standard of living as a student has always informally existed for a successful person: if you don't learn, you will be out of the window at some point. We must now focus on the decryption of the mechanisms of evolutionary learning and then show how everyone can perfect themselves. You can compare this to the genetic code: it has always existed, but it is only now being documented. The realization that innovative entrepreneurs who can survive well in the market economy can be produced will prevail.

Most entrepreneurship books are based on a high ideal of learning. But almost everyone tends to rely on tried and tested methods instead of constantly questioning everything, and above all, themselves.

But we need to look at entrepreneurship and the act of being an entrepreneur in a more practical light.

People who have had long-term success are the ones who belong to the category of entrepreneurs who are always learning. They are reflective, very self-critical, and have high emotional quality. Incidentally, quality also shows in defeat. If someone considers himself the greatest and the best, the zenith has passed, and the decline has begun. That is a very pragmatic attitude.

Entrepreneurship doesn't always go against the tried and tested patterns. They just seek hidden value in it.

BIOGRAPHY

Asmait Yohannes is an award-winning author, entrepreneur, accomplished leader, and founder of Asmait Skin Care. She brings collective business knowledge, financial expertise, and dynamic leadership success to the table. As a woman entrepreneur, Asmait's primary goal and passion are to help bring out the natural beauty in every woman and provide empowerment and inspiration to women worldwide by sharing the timeless pearls of wisdom of her ancestors. Asmait is driven by her belief: Beauty is Organic.

Connect with Asmait Yohannes via https://linktr.ee/asmait07

CHAPTER 7

Congratulations! I Just Want To Say Congratulations!

By Bryce Ball

Start Now. RIGHT NOW!

"Mom, I want a paper route," I told my mom when I was eight years old (in the third grade) because my nine-year-old friend from school had a paper route and made money. So, being eight, I wanted to start earlier than him. "Why do you want a paper route?" my mom asked. "Because I want a record player and a bike," I replied. When I first wanted these things, my mom told me that I would need money to get them. I was ready to earn, and the paper route was the best, and perhaps the only, option for an eight-year-old.

I delivered the *Las Vegas Review Journal* and later the *Las Vegas Sun* newspaper for ten years: from the age of eight to eighteen, right up to my high school graduation. I was able to buy my record player and bike a few months into my paper route, and I was also able to purchase many other things along the way. I kept a cash logbook to track my monthly profits. In retrospect, this was my first entrepreneurial experience and the foundation for my business ownership.

The first principle to take away from this story is that if you want something, get started as soon as possible. What I mean to say is don't waste your time contemplating, evaluating, considering, analyzing, etc. All those things just lead to what's commonly called analysis paralysis.

Just do it! Right now! There is no time to waste. Life is short. Your age, education level, race, gender, any external obstacles—none of those things matter. The *only* thing that matters is 'Start Now. Right Now!'

Learn Sales Skills

My mom laid the job section of a classified ad in front of me with one ad circled. It read as follows:

Cust Serv   Sporting Goods
(phone number)
FT/PT $11/Start

I was home for the summer after my sophomore year in college. During this time, my life would take an amazing turn. I figured this job would involve answering the phone and handling customer service calls for sports equipment, just as the ad implied. But during the interview, I learned that it was a position for selling Cutco Cutlery. At the time, I wasn't too sure if I was interested in selling knives. I was skeptical all through the interview, even after it was done. Then, I was accepted for the position in the follow-up interview.

I was trying to figure out every excuse to skip training day because I did not want to go. But I eventually, somewhat hesitantly, went. The training flowed smoothly. Ultimately, I was glad I went. We role-played the presentation, made a contact list, practiced our phone script, and were tasked with setting fifteen appointments for the following week. We learned the prices of all the knives (and they were expensive), how to present the price, build the product's value, cover the lifetime warranty, ask for the order, handle objectives, and get referrals. Then, off I went to sell knives beginning with my practice presentations. It definitely went pretty well for me, and we were very well trained.

I set two goals to achieve that summer. Firstly, I wanted to buy a new car. I had a picture of an IROC Z-28 on my wall all summer.

Secondly, I wanted to earn an opportunity for a company trip to Ixtapa, Mexico. I accomplished both of these goals that summer.

A few years later, I became a manager. In our training, they would always highlight that this experience would benefit us more along the lines of learning sales skills over the income one could make. I used to say that too, albeit half-heartedly because I was unsure how much I believed it to be true. Looking back on all those experiences I gained then, they were priceless. The same goes for anyone who took it seriously. Because of my time at this company, all my career moves have been made with individuals I met there. It was truly the best experience of my life, and it really taught me sales and sales management.

In Malcolm Gladwell's book, *The Outliers*, he talks about 10,000 hours to *hone your craft*. This means working on your skill: trials and errors; improving on it; getting better at it; learning from mistakes and not repeating them; and becoming the best you can be. All of these relate to sales skills. We are all in sales; everything we do is sales. If you spend time learning the art of selling, you will earn a great deal of income. But more importantly, you will understand the art of reading people, working with diverse personality types, building relationships, matching and mirroring, and helping people get what they want.

Lead by Example

My favorite human being on this planet is my six-year-old godson, Chase. I adore and love this little guy. His attitude is the best, and I love his personality. When I was to make the final phone call concerning my book and having it published, I told him, "Hey. I have this very important call that I need to focus on. Don't interrupt me, okay? Not until I'm off this call. And then, we can do whatever you want." After I got done with the call, he said, "Come here. Come into my room. I want to tell you something." I walked into his room, and he said, "Congratulations!! I just want to say congratulations. That's it." Then he hugged me. I replied, "Thanks, buddy," as I returned the hug. I literally have tears in my eyes as

I write this. It was really cool coming from him because he was so excited for me. This little guy is awesome.

Another one of our cute exchanges, one that I have often been practicing with him since he was two years old, goes as follows: "Say this with me. I am a leader!! Say it loud." He would reply: "I am a leader!" I'd ask him: "How do you lead?" He'd reply: "Lead by example." To this, I would reply: "That's right, buddy." I have him say this all the time.

I think this is an essential key to success. To me, this is what leadership is. Leadership is not 'Do what I say," but it's 'Do what I do.' We must be willing to get into the trenches with them and let them shadow us and learn. Anybody who is not willing to do this will not be a respected leader. You become a greater leader, especially a respected leader, when you lead by example.

Have an Open Mind

It was July 2016, and we were on our way to the Orange County Fair. We planned on a fun night of rides, games, and some good fairground food. I was with Chase, and his mother, Toye. Before we headed out to the fair, Toye told me about this new, confusing thing called Bitcoin. She was trying to explain this imaginary, digital money to me. She introduced me to this website where you could broker deals to help people obtain Bitcoin through various means of transfer. Toye had previously dabbled in Bitcoin, but that was the first night she had deposited some Bitcoin. She was offering people the ability to purchase Bitcoin, and depending on the medium of exchange, there was a nice margin of profit for her.

An hour later and before we even got into the fair, she sold all her Bitcoin and made a few hundred dollars. 'Well, that's cool,' I thought, but I wanted to get to the fair. We rode many rides and played a lot of games. We had a fantastic time, but I couldn't help but think about this Bitcoin thing the whole night.

Over the next several months, Toye taught me all about this amazing technology; she kept making exchanges and earning more money. Within a few months, I was into it as well. The world of cryptocurrency was fascinating. Toye has since become a Bitcoin Certified Professional and trades Bitcoin and Altcoins as her primary source of income. I have heavily invested in cryptocurrency and keep a daily pulse on this exciting industry.

Regarding this, Toye has often told me, "I tell you something, and you don't believe it until one of your guy friends tells you about it or validates it." She says it a little more forcefully and with slightly different terminology. But suffice to say, she was telling the truth. I have often not heeded her advice and ignored some things that would have worked out well for me. Because of this, I lost out on some potentially major opportunities. Fortunately, I heeded her advice when it came to Bitcoin and kept a more open mind.

I think that we are all hard-headed in general. Unless we think an idea is ours or have shared the idea with someone, we tend to resist it. This is a crucial success principle that needs to be applied more often. Someone's age or gender does not matter when it comes to giving advice. I find it very common that males, especially, put up a barrier when females advise them. This is also seen when someone younger than us offers us advice. Our initial reaction is, "Oh, come on. What do you know that I already don't know?" This is our egos getting in the way.

I have overcome that view. Now I maintain an open mind and heed advice from whoever it may be.

Invest in Yourself

Mentors and being under the tutelage of a mastermind plays a crucial role in our personal development. For the longest time, I had difficulty calling someone "My Mentor." I pictured this one gray-haired individual with a beard who was a wise old sage and would share all his wisdom with me. But what I found is that we have many mentors placed before us. They come in different forms and fashions. We must put our ego on a shelf and be willing to listen to the many insights we get from people out there.

I attended my first seminar (with Jim Rohn) back in 1992. It was one of the best seminars I've attended. Attending that first seminar gave me the desire and thirst to strive towards working on my personal development. I firmly believe that this is something we *need* in our life; call it fuel for the mind or gas for the soul. We should often recharge ourselves with events. I am currently part of several different mastermind groups where we interact with highly successful individuals, many of whom have a net worth of millions of dollars. One of the biggest values of these groups is the people with whom you connect and become friends. Tremendous value can be gained from these relationships.

People often ask me, "Since you are already successful, why would you go to these events and *pay* tens of thousands of dollars for this mentorship?" Why? These are the two primary reasons.

Firstly, we are either growing or dying. Secondly, we need to surround ourselves with people who make more money and have more knowledge than us—that is if we desire to continue making more money and reaching higher levels of success.

Begin *somewhere* would be my suggestion. Invest an amount that stretches you a bit. When the investment causes some pain, you will take it way more seriously. You will also be sure to get the value and your money's worth from the event or the group you join. Invest in yourself, and you will continually grow and become the best version of yourself.

In summary, these five success principles have helped guide my life and get me to my current level of success. Our growth throughout life can be exponential and give momentum to our careers and opportunities when we apply these principles.

1. Start Now. RIGHT NOW!

2. Learn Sales Skills

3. Lead by Example

4. Keep an Open Mind

5. Invest in Yourself

If you apply these principles in your life, you will be well on your way to your personal success. And I just want to say to you, as my godson, Chase, said to me: Congratulations! I just want to say congratulations!

BIOGRAPHY

Bryce Ball is a seasoned sales professional and entrepreneur with over thirty years of experience in sales and business ownership. For the last twenty years, he has been in the home furnishings and home improvement industry. Currently, he is the co-owner of a large national cabinet company. He has been responsible for over $100 million in sales throughout his organizations. His love for personal development over the last thirty years makes him an expert in transferring that knowledge to others and mentoring individuals to become the best version of themselves. A big kid at heart, much of his passion is towards teaching kids concepts not taught in our traditional school systems—teaching our youth to think like an entrepreneur and develop their confidence through personal development. His hobbies include most sports, and he is a worldwide traveler, especially if there is a beach involved.

Connect with Bryce Ball via https://linktr.ee/bryceball

CHAPTER 8

Black Belts Never Quit Or Give Up!

By Master Chris Lee DeSherlia

It was March 2020, and I was just getting ready to close on my first house. I was excited and apprehensive at the same time. I felt like all the information and paperwork required of me was like asking for my left arm and firstborn. The seller had the foresight to simply sign all the paperwork and leave as soon as he closed on the property. After I got the keys to my new house, the governor of Illinois spoke of Covid-19 and was apparently suggesting I close my business or reduce its overall capacity. The national news talked about shutting down everything to stabilize this virus spiraling out of control in some countries. I was naïve in thinking it wouldn't come to such a massive nationwide shutdown of many small mom-and-pop-run businesses.

I planned to reduce the class sizes to the recommended eight or less (as prescribed by the CDC), and I was on the "business parents" page posting the new proposed class times for each rank and the breakdown of the ages. Then, the news came in that all businesses, except those deemed essential, would be shut down, including all daycares, schools, and colleges. Luckily, I was involved with many martial arts school owners across the country and noticed they were pivoting towards an online learning platform, so I dove right in myself. Most of the martial arts schools across the country were using Zoom or other platforms like Microsoft Teams.

I watched my income dwindle rather rapidly as there were cancellations upon cancellations; fear and panic took hold of most of my student body. People everywhere were losing their jobs, as restaurants and fast-food joints could no longer offer indoor dining. During this time, I became depressed and wondered if this was just a bad dream from which I would one day wake up. I spent much of my life learning martial arts, and now I was even being denied my business interruption insurance claim. I couldn't believe my lifeline was being pulled away from me at the time I needed it the most. A core group of supporters believed in my mission for the school and encouraged me to persevere.

I remember when I decided to keep the doors open, no matter what, and I remember the talk I had with the kids and parents when I quit Zoom classes in June 2020. After about two-and-a-half months of only having myself and another black belt student teach online classes, we were finally able to offer in-person training. I taped off the training areas for social distancing; no contact was allowed except on the kicking bags. I even revamped the curriculum. Lucky for me, I had two entrances and exits. I made the back entrance the only entrance, and the front entrance was an exit only. I also kept all the dressing/changing rooms off-limits, and the bathrooms were for emergency use only. I set up sanitizing stations throughout the school, required masks for entry and exit, and no parents were allowed in the building to watch. I announced my plan to the parents' group and was reassured and thanked for keeping everyone safe and protected. My classes were reduced to thirty minutes to allow students to flow in and out and give us time to disinfect and wipe down the equipment for the next group of eight or less. Once the in-person classes began, I gave a speech to all my junior mixed belts and those of higher ranks. I told them I could have closed my doors like everyone else, but what would that have taught them about perseverance, persistence, overcoming challenges, and becoming a black belt? Also, what kind of example or role model would I be? I watched the news and noticed on Facebook that a lot of other martial arts schools around the country were closing their doors for good or struggling to pay their leases. I knew I had to persevere and carry on so my legacy wouldn't die from something I couldn't control. I chose to control how I would respond to it.

I always carry a gold credit-looking card in my wallet to this day that says, '**Don't Ever Give Up!**' It has a picture of a stork or pelican eating a frog, and the frog's webbed hands strangling the stork's neck, refusing to be swallowed.

Every time I think about throwing in the towel, quitting, or just giving up, I pull out that gold card and meditate on it as well as the poem on the back. I love the proverb, 'Success is failure turned inside out.' When things seem at their worst, you must not quit. If not for the martial arts discipline that was instilled in me at such a young age, I would have thrown in the towel many times. Most people don't know this about me, and this might be the first time I have laid my soul bare: I've lost and failed more times than I can remember. I tried selling home alarm systems. I sold new and used cars. I attempted to sell oil change and auto repair franchises. Every time I did something that wasn't martial-arts-related, a former student or instructor would pull me back into teaching. They would ask me for advice, or they would somehow track me down to ask a martial-arts-related question or just check up on me. When I was doing something that wasn't martial arts related, like selling cars or something, they would tell me I had a gift for teaching martial arts. I've made many friends, mentors, training partners, coaches, and acquaintances throughout my martial arts journey. I believe in guardian angels because my guardian angel has protected me, shielded me, and made me realize that my biggest gift is helping people become empowered to face whatever life throws at them.

I had my storage shed broken into in the early 1990s, and my collectibles were stolen: $50,000 worth of comics, collectible cards, and such. I sold the building in which my father used to teach to a friend of a student. They lied to me and took $5,000 worth of materials I paid for but never received. I lost our family house because my father's friend lied to the bank and had it foreclosed and ended up paying the bank instead of me since it was a contract of deed. I've had my share of setbacks, heartaches, and failures.

I left my former boss due to a family emergency back home in Illinois. My grandfather had Alzheimer's, and it was getting worse, and I didn't want to have any regrets about not being able to say goodbye. Once I came back to Illinois, I applied for different jobs in retail and such. I also helped my step-grandma, Edith, take care of my grandpa during his bout with Alzheimer's. I would come over, keep him company, and sit and talk to him. One night, late in October, while I was at my friend's house, watching the Alton Halloween parade, I got a call from Edith. She was frantic and didn't know what to do. My grandpa had collapsed on the floor, and Edith couldn't get him up. So, I left the parade, as it was winding down anyway. I ended up staying the night, so I could help Edith if grandpa fell again. My grandpa, Claude, had just started his new medication recommended by the doctor. He showed all the side effects of the new medicine, which Edith, who was of German descent, tried to explain to the doctors. I was able to let Claude's doctor understand that the medication was doing more harm than good, in addition to the fact that it was being discontinued in Europe due to its harmful side effects. During the pandemic, I felt the sadness and grief of all those who couldn't or wouldn't be able to say goodbye to their loved ones. I saw the open burial pits in New York, where bodies were just being put in mass graves. Such a tragedy.

They say when the student is ready, the teacher will appear. This has happened twice in my lifetime. The first was when I was a fourth-degree black belt in Taekwondo (TKD). During this time, I felt stagnant like still water, as far as my martial arts development was concerned, neither moving nor flowing but just going through the motions. I was getting ready to teach a class, and one of my black belts came in with a flyer from the local health club regarding Filipino Martial Arts (FMA). I had heard of FMA through the grapevine and casual mentions about Bruce Lee's training. Out of curiosity, I went to see this teacher and was able to have a pleasant, casual conversation about the mindset of an attacker with a bladed weapon. I was impressed not only with this gentleman's knowledge and expertise but the literal scars of his experience. I ended up training privately with Guro Jimmy Tacosa for about a year. I ended up incorporating FMA and especially Tacosa Serrada Escrima into my TKD curriculum and ended up having a great deal of success in the open martial arts tournament scene. The FMA helped me increase my hand speed, hand-eye coordination, and development of something called the "flow." It's what Escrimadors describe as being able to feel, sense, and properly respond in relation to your opponent's openings, blocks, attacks, and counters without a sense of panic or dread. A calmness overcomes you mentally, physically, and spiritually. That seems almost too simple to naturally explain as it encompasses a higher level of consciousness. My instructor left the area for personal reasons, which left a void in my life for a while. I persevered and continued my training. However, it just wasn't the same, and the distance commitment was much further than before. A few years ago, I ended up testing for my Tacosa Serrada Escrima Level I Instructorship under this instructor and completing one of my goals, which I wanted to achieve before his passing away (he is still alive today).

My second teacher was a TKD instructor who also studied Chinese Kung Fu and Israeli hand-to-hand combat. If Bruce Lee's spirit of being a workaholic and striving for constant and never-ending improvement was alive, this man has it in spades. Master Trento has a cane, and most of the time, he walks with a slight limp, like a wise old sage. Yet, he's already outlived his doctor's prognosis of not making it past thirty years. Seriously, the difference in his mannerisms, once he begins to teach, is like turning on a light switch. Passion is an understatement; the man is on fire. He has an agenda to download as much knowledge as you can soak up from his training stories, deep-level research, and personal experience from his instructors, current and former. He has notebooks filled with daily workouts, lesson plans, and evolving techniques tested under stress-like lab conditions. I have been fortunate enough to become a certified instructor and have an affiliate combat TKD school.

Both these gentlemen have helped me develop as a martial artist physically, mentally, and spiritually. Every time I think about quitting, giving up, or throwing in the towel, I think about the hardships and sacrifices these two endured to leave a legacy for the future. Remember that a black belt is just a white belt who never quit. Don't give up on your goals, dreams, and wishes. Realize that everybody is fighting a private battle for something or someone. I hope you get some nuggets of inspiration to help you on your journey of becoming the best you.

BIOGRAPHY

Master Chris Lee DeSherlia is a Korean American author, entrepreneur, speaker, coach, and certified self-defense instructor in Combat TKD and COBRA. He began his martial arts training at the young age of four under his father, Great Grandmaster Yi In Soo. He has trained under various grandmasters in TKD, including Sung Chae Kim, Won Kuk Kim, Kim Bok Man, and his uncle Pyo. He has also taken seminars and workshops from celebrity martial artists like Dan Inosanto, Bill Wallace, and Joe Lewis. He has taken his lifelong passion for martial arts, combining it with fitness and strength conditioning. His teaching encompasses life skills such as focus, discipline, determination, goal setting, and respect. Master "Chris Lee's" mission is to empower lives through martial arts training and build a community of positive role models, "One Black Belt at a Time." "Pil Sung" is his favorite Korean phrase, which translated means, "I am certain of victory!"

Connect with Master Chris Lee DeSherlia via https://linktr.ee/kjnchris

CHAPTER 9

Never Forget

By David Dubis

As I approached the bathroom at BestBuy, I asked myself: Which one will be worse? The male bathroom or the female bathroom? How many clogged toilets am I going to find? Will there be any surprises to encounter this day?

That was my job back then. Yes. My job: cleaning bathrooms at BestBuy. But I wasn't limited to just bathrooms, but also the floors and carpeting in the store.

When I came to the USA for the first time, from my native country, Venezuela, my first job was at my uncle's and aunt's cleaning company in Miami, FL. They had many clients, one of whom was the BestBuy near their house. In addition to BestBuy, I cleaned the floors and bathrooms of schools, gas stations, office spaces, nursing homes, and many other places.

Going back to the time when I began questioning what I was doing cleaning the bathroom at BestBuy, I was picking up used toilet paper from the floor. Disgusted with the smell, I asked myself another set of questions: What am I doing here? Is this why I came to the US? How long will I be doing this? I felt that this was the lowest point of my life because I was reduced to cleaning bathrooms. Keep in mind that these bathrooms were quite dirty and messy. I don't want to disgust you with any more details, but I'm sure you get the picture.

I worked this job because I was helping my family pay for the paperwork and fees required to immigrate to the US.

As I approached the next bathroom, I heard a voice in my head. It was my father's voice, telling me: "Son, never forget where you came from."

I came from a beach town called Puerto La Cruz on the coast of Venezuela. I experienced a great childhood there. When I was sixteen, I came to the US. My mother is from Colombia. She is the daughter of two immigrants who fled to Venezuela in the seventies when she was fifteen years old because of the political and social turmoil that went on in Colombia. My father is the son of two European immigrants. My grandfather fought the Nazis in World War II when they invaded his home country, Poland. My grandfather's war stories are simply unbelievable, but I'll save those for the next book. I'll tell you this, though. When the draft took place in Poland, young boys had to either work or join the military. My grandfather chose the military and fought in the war for several years. But one of his friends, the goalkeeper on his soccer team, chose to work; he later joined the seminary to become a Catholic Priest. That young man was Karol Józef Wojtyła, who became the first non-Italian to hold the highest position in the Catholic Church since the sixteenth century. He was Pope John Paul II. I always say, tongue in cheek, that my grandfather could have become the Pope.

Moving onto my work in the US, I continued to work in the same field—cleaning bathrooms and floors—for a few years. Then, I enrolled at a community college to learn English. After completing the program, I obtained a position at BestBuy. This time, it wasn't bathrooms; I was a loss prevention associate. I enjoyed that job, and I was good at it. I continued my education at the community college, taking up a film production program because I always wanted to become an actor or filmmaker. I began developing friendships and expanding my social circle, which began to greatly increase. I would go out to nightclubs and party till very early in the morning. This affected my work performance at BestBuy, and I was eventually fired.

Nightlife got the better of me, as I was never on my best behavior. I dropped out of the film production program. I did not have enough money to even fill gas in my car. I kept asking my father for money until one day he told me that I had to do something with my life—and I had to do it quickly. If not, he would kick me out of his house. The year was 2007, and I was twenty-one years old at the time. I was once again desperate and felt like I was at my lowest point; I was depressed and had no purpose. So, I found my way to a recruiting station for the US Army. They wanted me to sign the papers right away. I did not want that, and I left. Following this, I entered the Navy's recruiting office and had an entirely different experience. I had to take a test and look out for openings. I took the test and chose my job. I became a firefighter. It was an awesome job.

So, I was sent to boot camp at RTC, Great Lakes, IL. And I found myself cleaning bathrooms and floors again. It was a shock, and I thought to myself, 'What! Not again!' But this time, the voice in my head kept repeating itself, "Never forget where you came from." It began motivating me little by little.

On the brighter side of things, I was the best at cleaning the bathrooms and floors, so I was constantly praised for it. All the training and sacrifice in my uncle's company helped me to achieve this.

In November 2007, I graduated second in my class. My family, especially my parents, were very proud of me that day. I was elated and felt motivated to do many great things in the Navy. Following this, I went to specialty school and graduated first in my class. I was extremely happy and filled with pride. I received my first command orders; I was stationed on a destroyer in Pearl Harbor, HI. "I am going to Hawaii!" I said, with the biggest smile on my face. After a few weeks there, the Navy flew me to my ship, which began its deployment to the Persian Gulf. There I was, a crew member of a billion-dollar warship—the mighty USS RUSSELL (DDG59). Everything went great: I was training, learning my job well, advancing quickly, and received a couple of awards and a rank advance. My first deployment was finished, and we returned to Hawaii for a well-deserved vacation. On that vacation, I decided to marry my girlfriend, Wendy, who was waiting for me in Miami. We got married and went to live in Hawaii. Life was amazing, and we were happy—a dream come true for both of us.

Three months after our wedding, the USS RUSSELL was scheduled for another deployment: this would be my second deployment to the Middle East. It was quite long and rough, almost ten months. I hardly got the chance to speak to my wife over the phone; I was limited to letters and emails whenever that was possible. We carried out many missions, including a rescue mission for a Somalian boat that had seventy people on board, including women and children. Not everyone survived that mission, and some of the folks and children had to be thrown into the ocean. It was pretty hard to see that, but these stories are for another book.

I was stronger and prouder because of all the sacrifices I was making. Serving my country and loved ones gave me a great deal of pride. After coming back, I took a five-month vacation, following which was my third deployment. This one was very hard because I was without my wife for three years.

As I embarked on the USS RUSSELL for my third and last deployment on that ship, I reflected on the ship's motto. Every ship had a motto, but I never paid attention to the meaning. "Strength forged through sacrifice" was the RUSSELL's motto. I was sad, leaving my wife behind. But after reflecting on the motto, that voice spoke to me again: "SON! Never forget where you came from." It gave me the push I needed to keep moving forward.

The third deployment was brutal: lots of work, lots of exercise, and long hours (sixteen-to-nineteen-hour workdays). I was sleeping four hours a day—that was when I was lucky. This really took a toll on me, and it felt like a prison. My relationship with my wife was also affected due to all the time I spent away. When I returned, I was highly irritable, and my mood was just not right. But I kept reflecting back on the ship's motto and my dad's voice.

As soon as I got home, I was transferred to Norfolk, VA, to be part of another ship's crew: the USS NEW YORK (LPD21). I won't deny that I was excited to be part of another trip, but I was depressed at the same time. I lost two of my good friends from the USS RUSSELL, and my best friend in Miami committed suicide. This significantly impacted and demotivated me. The new ship, which would be my home for the next three years, would take me on my fourth deployment. I was once again sad and felt that I had no purpose. Also, my marriage was going downhill.

I remember walking towards the ship as I embarked on it for the first time. I saw the ship's motto on a huge banner spread across the quarterdeck. It read, "NEVER FORGET." At that moment, I was in awe and also in a bit of shock. I could not believe that my father's words were my new ship's motto. At this moment, I found strength in all the sacrifices I made all this time. At the beginning of 2011, the ship made its maiden deployment. The tour was to last for nine months. The tour was amazing, filled with great missions and accomplishments. I was the main instructor on the ship, and I trained enlisted personnel, officers, and marines who were on board. By the end of 2011, I was placed in the top ten percent of the Navy, giving me the opportunity to teach new sailors at RTC, Great Lakes, IL. Life was great. Everything made sense to me. I had a purpose once again.

As I prepared to become an instructor, I was facing issues with my marriage. The long hours at school, lack of communication, and my irritability played a major role in all that. Throughout my time as an instructor, I had the opportunity to personally train over 30,000 service members. I made public speeches before hundreds of people and government officials. It was definitely an amazing learning experience for me.

In 2013, my tour as an instructor came to an end, and I transitioned to the civilian sector. It took about a year as I struggled to adapt and relate to average people again. My marriage was falling to pieces, and my dog died. I was once again hopeless and without purpose. My family played a major role in supporting me during this time. I can never thank them for all that they have done for me. I am truly blessed to have them in my life.

Then, something marvelous happened. I was going to be a father. YES! We had a beautiful baby girl named Alanah. Once again, I found motivation and my purpose in life. I landed a marketing job in a very good company in Miami. My father's voice continued to resonate in my head, saying: "Never forget where you came from." That voice kept me motivated, picked me up from the ground, and pretty much kept me alive.

I became an entrepreneur and continued to help families and businesses. I am stronger because of all the sacrifices I made, and I will never forget how I got to this point. It seems like it was only yesterday when my father took me to that mountain in our beach town in Venezuela and showed me the city, lights, and buildings, saying: "Son! You are going to the USA. You will do great things. But I want to tell you this. Never forget where you came from." You see, those words were so deep that it wasn't until recently that I understood what my father meant. My life has now taken an amazing turn as I'm becoming a more successful entrepreneur every day. But this is also for the next book.

I will leave you with these words from Oprah Winfrey: "If you look at what you have in life, you'll always have more. If you look at what you don't have in life, you'll never have enough."[4]

BIOGRAPHY

David Dubis is a US Navy veteran with four deployments to the Middle East under his belt. As an instructor and mentor, David has personally trained and motivated over 30,000 people from many backgrounds and ages, earning his placement in the top ten percent of the Navy. A father of a beautiful three-year-old girl, he loves to spend time with family and helping others in his community through different charity programs that help the less fortunate, one of which feeds over 700 children in remote villages in his native country, Venezuela. Now, as an entrepreneur, David

---

4   Quotespedia.org, "If You Look at What You Have in Life, You'll Always Have More. - Oprah Winfrey," Quotespedia.org, April 8, 2020, https://www.quotespedia.org/authors/o/oprah-winfrey/if-you-look-at-what-you-have-in-life-youll-always-have-more-oprah-winfrey/.

continues to serve his country by helping families and business owners protect themselves by getting access to legal representation across the US and Canada. David believes that everyone deserves equal access to the legal system. His motivation and vision are to mentor more people around him to experience massive success in their business and personal life. The most important part of success is not the result, but rather the journey that gets you there.

Connect with David Dubis via https://linktr.ee/daviddubis

CHAPTER 10

Surviving Isn't Good Enough

By DaVonda St. Clair

I don't ever recall having a rock bottom moment, but I've had several *bottom* moments at different points in my life. We've all hit such moments, but how you deal with them is the true testament. A testament to your character. A testament to your strength and courageousness. A testament to being a survivor. A testament to *you*.

One of my bottom moments happened during a bubble bath.

I love taking bubble baths—soaking, relaxing, reflecting, with or without music, with or without candles. During this particular bath, I found myself feeling anxious. Then, I started sulking, which turned into sobbing, and then ugly crying. These overwhelming emotions came crashing down over me after a period of being extremely optimistic about my situation. Why could I not land a job? It had been three months since I last worked. I thought landing another contract role in the Middle East would be easier the second go around. Besides, I had a graduate degree and professional work experience. I was familiar with the Middle Eastern work environment. I am also a veteran. So, why was it hard to secure another job?

After working in Qatar for a year and a half, I decided not to renew my contract with that company. The contract company lowballed everyone: low pay, one day off a week, and too much employee drama. I didn't make a ton of money, but I managed to save plenty. The company paid for furnished accommodations, supplied a vehicle, a gas card, and phone cards to add minutes to our company-provided phone. The only out-of-pocket expense we had was food, usually dinner and meals during our one day off. I took the position in Qatar to get my foot in the door working as a Defense Department contractor. Having work experience in the Middle East, I figured it should be easier to land another job with my qualifications, work experience, being a veteran, and having familiarity with working in the region. While working in Qatar, I tried strategizing how I would transition from a career in logistics to the realm of technology. My degrees were a Bachelor's in Computer Information Systems and a Master's in Information Technology Management. Surely, I could land a role in technology. But how?

After returning to the United States, I stayed with my grandmother. I didn't exactly tell her I was out of work. Maybe she thought I was back home visiting for a vacation. I never said anything different. Every morning, I would get up early, make sure I was dressed, and out the door with my laptop in tow, either going to the library or any place with free Wi-Fi to search and apply for jobs in the Middle East. A few weeks went by, I received emails of "potential offers," but nothing solid. I thought landing a job would be so much easier with my credentials; nothing materialized. Looking for a job is seriously a full-time job in itself, especially when you are networking from scratch and with no real point of reference. After job-hunting all day, I would go back to my grandmother's before nightfall, watch television, and converse. A month went by, and my grandmother finally asked when I would be returning to work. I took that as me having overstayed my welcome. I answered by saying I was leaving in a few days to visit some friends. The next day, I took to social media and emails to plan a trip "visiting" friends and family while I was still searching for a job.

As it worked out, it was mid-May summertime. People were taking days off, and kids were home from school/college, so it was the perfect time to schedule "visits" to folks I hadn't seen in a while—especially with those who didn't mind me having a cat. Yes, a cat. My feline pet companion of six years was with me, "couch surfing." Some nights, we would stay in hotels. Fortunately, I had money saved up to where we didn't have to sleep in the car. This went on for another month—Illinois, Ohio, Virginia, North Carolina, Georgia, to Louisiana. Louisiana was the last stop. I stayed here for thirty days. Here is where the meltdown happened.

Recruiters were calling me back, but the companies weren't immediately winning contracts. Therefore, jobs were not instantly available. They would ask me to wait, but I wasn't willing to wait until September or October, let alone January or February. I wanted something that would have me leave almost immediately. Nothing turned up. The friend I visited in Louisiana had just gone through a divorce, so he had an extra room for me and my cat. This was a godsend, as I was draining my savings. After staying there for a few weeks, he went on a trip out of town for the weekend, so I had the house to myself. That's when I decided to take a relaxing bubble bath.

Bubble baths usually soothed me and often provided clarity to my many thoughts. I began to cry, then sob. The sobbing I experienced was like no other. I sobbed from disappointment, shame, and embarrassment— sobbing because I felt like a failure. The bathroom door was ajar. I noticed it widened a bit as my cat walked in and jumped on the edge of the tub as though he was saying, "I am here." He then laid next to the tub until I collected my emotions, after which I got out of the tub and dressed for bed. That night, after ugly, ugly sobbing, I felt relief. Maybe it was all the emotions I bottled up for months.

Almost every day for two-and-a-half months, I researched companies, spoke to recruiters, revamped my resume, and applied for jobs. Whoever came up with the phrase, "Looking for a full-time job *is* a full-time job," must have gone through this same process. A week after my friend returned from his vacation, he commented on helping him pay half the mortgage if I decided to stay. My focus was living and working abroad, having a fun life, travel, excitement, joy, and the mood of YOLO (You Only Live Once). Not to live in Louisiana or anywhere stateside. That fueled my determination, even more, to find a job abroad quickly.

Finding a job in the Middle East from the US was hard. I knew if I did it once, I could do it again. My goal was to live abroad; I never wavered from that. Although momentarily, I thought, 'Will I have to take a job in the US?' I figured if I did that, I would lose focus or not be as ambitious working toward returning overseas.

A few days after his comment, a recruiter called, looking to fill a position in the Kingdom of Bahrain. I didn't recall applying for a position there, but it was a possible opportunity. The call immediately led to a job offer. I was able to negotiate a good salary. The additional benefits provided were almost the same as the last company I worked for, but *better—much better*! Landing this job offer felt like a huge weight lift off of me. I was to leave as soon as I completed all the required pre-travel/pre-employment documentation. YES! YES! YES! I was relieved, ecstatic, and ready to go. The only thing I truly remember was taking Caesar (my cat) to the veterinarian for his export/import exam for us to travel internationally. Not only was this perfect timing, but the position was also for an Information Technology (IT) Asset Manager, a position that would eventually lead me to a career in IT. From my experiences, I am now in a position to help others successfully transition into IT or find employment internationally.

I never wavered from my vision or goal to live and work abroad. Nor was I ever afraid. Moving abroad presents so many opportunities for personal growth, cultural knowledge, spirituality, and expanding your social circle. I knew I could live a much better and fulfilled life abroad because it was a different environment, bustling with a lifestyle and opportunities unavailable in the United States. This vision started early, while in junior high school, going on school trips, and watching the travel channel and the TV shows *Lifestyles of the Rich & Famous* and *The Fabulous life of . . . .* I would often imagine visiting, eating the foods, speaking with the locals, and sightseeing at the destinations where the *Travel Channel* would take me. The other two shows displayed the luxury and decadence of people's actual lives. I figured, if they could do it, I could do too. I placed myself in those magnificent homes, driving exotic cars, flying around the world, having a charmed life, loving it, and being grateful for it. Imagining . . . it wasn't until I was older did I realize that imagining, playing out your dreams by walking through those neighborhoods you envision living in when you grow up, sitting in the driver's seat of that fancy car one of your relatives owned or at the car dealership, is the same as visualizing. Little did we know those adults encouraging us to imagine, dream, and play dress-up were encouraging us to visualize what is possible, where we could be, what we could do, and who we could become.

My service in the military deepened my longing to live abroad. I lived and traveled throughout the United States. But living in Panama and South Korea was incredible. We constantly ventured throughout Panama and South Korea and soaked up and interacted with the culture. Not only did we "live" in these countries, but we also thrived. Again, we explored not only the touristy spots but also the ones which the locals enjoyed (those that were not "off-limits"). We were living day to day and having fun. Being in the United States, we tend to live day to day, take our hometown for granted, not venturing around the city, learning about it, discovering what's interesting, and finding out what's historic. Not many people take the time to explore their own city, let alone the state. Many fall into the mundane tasks of working, paying bills, living day-to-day, and finding a way to survive, not live. This time, not being military, I wanted to live and work overseas on my own terms, stay or venture off to another location based on my own desires.

That call in Louisiana sent me to live and work in the Middle East, in the Kingdom of Bahrain, where I found a community of Americans, various expatriates, and Bahrainis, all of whom thrived on culture, creativity, self-nourishment, enlightenment, and reflection. I thrived on being around a group of like-minded people. From this, a new definition of success was born. Everyone has a different definition of success. The question is: Are you living out your version of success? If not, why? An even better question is: do you know how?

One of my many mentors, Leon Howard (aka WallStreet Trapper), suggests people ask themselves these five questions:

1. Where do I want to be?

2. Where do I want to go?

3. What do I want to have?

4. Who am I going to help?

5. What am I going to give up?

Other mentors (Marcus Barney, HIM500, Circle of CEOs, etc.) and mentoring/self-development programs (Mr. Fire) I have been involved with always circle back to the same mantra of visualization. Visualize what you want. Visualize where you want to be. Visualize where you want to live. Visualize yourself helping others. Think it, breathe it, be it, and do it! It all begins with you. Tell your story. Remember that your story doesn't end when things don't work. It's simply the beginning. Visualize it. Live it. Thrive in it. Tell it.

BIOGRAPHY

DaVonda St.Clair is a poet, writer, and now co-author of Journey to Success. "I believe helping (people) comes in many forms. Whether it's sharing a warm smile that brightens a stranger's day, sharing your story which changes someone's life's path, or simply sitting still to listen." DaVonda has always advocated for self-development, community advancement, environmental initiatives, animal welfare, and human rights. She continues her commitment as well as her social responsibility through global philanthropic endeavors, including donating to and being involved with Feeding America, FreeMySister.Org, The Bahrain Writers Circle, Artists for a New South Africa (ANSA), American Women's League Kuwait, the Bahrain Society for the Prevention of Cruelty to Animals (BSPCA), and Protecting Animal Welfare Society (PAWS) Kuwait. DaVonda is also an International poet with published works in several books regarding the Kingdom of Bahrain, Sisterhood, Love, and International Living.

Connect with DaVonda St.Clair https://linktr.ee/DStClair

CHAPTER 11

Marine Veteran From Struggling To Winning

By Devin M. Davis

All my life, I wanted to do something great.

I've had hopes and dreams of doing things that were bigger than me and dreams of doing something bigger than anyone I knew, in my family, I was a dreamer for sure. I did not know how I was going to do anything great. I always thought I was here to win, trying to be the next best version of myself. I knew that being the best version of myself in my small city was not what I had in mind.

When I was seventeen, I could not wait to graduate so I could join the Marine Corps. I talked to a marine recruiter many times, and I didn't need much convincing that being a Marine was the only thing I wanted to do. I remember watching movies in high school like *Born on the Fourth of July* and *Full Metal Jacket*, and that is what I wanted to do. So, I joined the Marine Corps right out of high school. It was everything I wanted and needed in my life, and I loved it. I did my time, went on deployments, lived overseas, and traveled to many different countries. I was taught how to be a Marine, which was perfect and amazing, until the day I retired.

The Transition

Transitioning from military life after twenty years of service to being a civilian was one of the hardest things I've ever done—and I've done many hard things in the military. I was in the infantry. I was a grunt. That was a hard life. My job in the Marine Corps was to engage in combat on foot. We ran and hiked everywhere and anywhere. We trained for any fight. Life as a grunt was not easy. The struggle to transition to civilian life was very hard, very difficult. As I mentioned, I am a person who always wants to always be my best self. That all came to a halt when my life went from 100 miles an hour to zero. Life got slow, and it came to a halt. Time got slower. I was excited to retire from the Marine Corps but had no idea what life would be like once I became a civilian. I knew I had some PTSD, depression, and anxiety owing to my many years in the Marine Corps, but I did not think much of it. Let's just say when I tried to adapt to this new civilian life, my PTSD, depression, and anxiety got so bad that I didn't even want to leave the house. Doing normal things became a struggle, and all the things I enjoyed doing, like working out and going to the gym, were no longer enjoyable.

My Depression

My depression and anxiety were so crippling that I had to take a stand and be stronger than my mind. I really had to fight it to get better. I knew it would not be easy, but I was a marine . . . I was a fighter. But depression is a real thing. It is a deep feeling that is super hard to deal with. I was not the only one hurting from PTSD. I felt I had the duty to help others even though I was hurting. I noticed when I started to help other veterans who were worse off than me, I didn't think about my mental health issues as much. So, I decided to reach out to other veterans with the hard questions, but not directly. For example, I would ask them:

"Do you need a ride to any of your medical appointments?"
"Do you need help with any paperwork and financial advice?"
"Do you want to go to the gym tomorrow and work out?"

I was good at training people in the gym, and I was always good with documents, filling them out, and writing reports since I got stuck in company offices many a time typing reports and giving personal finance classes to younger marines. So, helping other veterans would actually help me with my struggles. I felt I had some purpose again, which enabled me to work on my transition. I was helping many veterans with various personal issues. I would help them in the gym, with their finances, and with their relationships. I'd also help them with any legal trouble they were having. I was doing a lot of good things for many of them—and for free—because that is what I felt I needed to do at the time. It was helping me with my struggle. My PTSD and depression were getting better, but I was financially broke.

I Was Broke

Not only was I financially broke, but I was also in debt with over $50,000 in bills and loans and lived in a horrible, super-small, overpriced apartment. I felt I should be further in life. I was losing big time. Something was *not* right. *This* was not right! I was tired of living in worry and fear all the time and just playing not to lose. I needed to fight for the person I was when I was seventeen years old, waiting to graduate high school so I could join the Marine Corps and live my dream. I wanted my dreams back. I wanted that hope again. I wanted to win again. I needed to win and fight to be the person I was born to be. It was the moment I felt awake and alive.

I got clarity on what I wanted and why. I could still help veterans and people and help myself financially at the same time. I could do this. I could still do something great, win at life, and be a person of influence. I got very focused and clear that I was going to play to win now. I was highly motivated to get out of debt, get out of that apartment, and buy a house. Another reason for this was that my girlfriend at the time wanted to have a family. She wanted to have a baby, and she deserved that.

Time to Win

How was I going to do this? How was I going to get out of debt and make my girlfriend proud of me and make me proud of me? I was seeing signs everywhere about starting a business and making passive income. Sales and marketing videos were popping up on YouTube. I saw this quote: "Your obsessions become your possessions." Very interesting. What am I good at? How can I make some serious wins? I started purely investing in myself with many personal development books such as *Think and Grow Rich*, *As A Man Thinketh*, and *The Secret* by Rhonda Byrne. From all the books I read, I knew that I could still grow a business and give back to people. So that is what I did. I really dug into the business of helping people with their financial issues. I remember years ago that I had a mentor who helped me with my finances and got me back on my feet during the recession of 2008. I could do that. I could help veterans, regular folks, or anyone who needed help with finances. But I need to build something quickly because I felt I was running out of time. My goal was to own a house, be debt-free, and have a successful company that would help people with their finances by the end of the year. So, I started going on the offense—REALLY DIGGING IN—and began to fight for my dream. Why not me? I think we all can win in life if we show some passion. I think we all deserve to have our dreams come true. I knew I was not the smartest person in the world, but I started to learn about business, sales, marketing, and technology. I learned anything was possible if I put my heart into it.

Within six months, and after making a ton of mistakes, getting knocked down, losing money on a deal, and having people still owe me money, I started to win. Small wins turned into big wins. I began to gain momentum, and in June 2020, I paid off all my debt. I saved enough money for a down payment for the house I always wanted. And about that house I always dreamt of? I got it!!

This is why you need to hustle. This is why you have to play offense. This is why you have to fight for yourself, your family, and your dream of always being the next best version of yourself. From struggling to winning, you can always have your hopes and dreams come true.

BIOGRAPHY

Devin M. Davis is a retired US Marine Veteran and self-made entrepreneur who has built several successful businesses, including a business coaching and financial services company. He is an expert in all matters of finance. He has taught and studied finance, credit, business, money, motivation, and leadership for many years. He is from the Los Angeles, CA area and graduated from Thousand Oaks High School in 1993. After graduating from high school, he quickly joined the Marine Corps because that was something he always wanted to do, which was being part of something greater than himself. While he was a marine, he took on many duties such as infantry, leadership, and mentoring many marines. He currently lives in San Diego, CA. After the Marine Corps, he decided to use his Post-911 GI Bill to complete his bachelor's degree in management. He graduated Cum Laude in September 2019.

Connect with Devin Davis via https://linktr.ee/DevinMDavis

CHAPTER 12

Keep Reading Your Story

By Emna Khechine, PhD

It was one week before the start of the academic year; the summer holidays were almost done. I was out for a long swim. This was not unusual for me because water is my element. As I approached the shores of the beach, I felt a sharp pain in my stomach. I was in great pain for a few minutes. Then, it left me all of a sudden.

"Mrs. Khechine, you have nothing except a slight case of anemia. I can prescribe you some iron tablets, vitamins, and an anti-depressor . . ." the doctor went on. He was not the first doctor to tell me this. I left the clinic and drove for hours, my head full of darkness. I was alone with my thoughts. 'Are you serious?! Nothing?! Then, why do I feel this pain in my body every morning? Why can I not wake up like a normal person? Why can't I concentrate during my lectures? And why do I faint so often?' I stopped by a supermarket, grabbed a large pack of chips, devoured the whole thing like an animal, and made my way to the university.

People would always gossip about me during those times. They even dared to calculate my average grade using some sophisticated software to determine whether or not I would pass. I'd be fine if they just ignored me. But as Jung said, "Thinking is difficult, that's why most people judge."[5]

---

5   "Thinking Is Difficult, That's Why Most People Judge.--Carl Jung by Mr Great Motivation," Mr Great Motivation, accessed July 6, 2021, https://www. mrgreatmotivation.com/2018/04/thinking-is-difficult-thats-why-most.html.

People talk about you when they don't have what you have, can't be like you, or when they can't reach out. The truth is *nobody* knows your story. *Nobody* is you. Nobody knows more about yourself than you do. So, you neither have to prove yourself to anyone nor do you have to change their minds about you.

Going back to my condition, receiving the same news from every doctor reached a point where I wished to spend the rest of my life in a clinic. One night, I remember crying to my mother and asking her: "Why is this happening to me? Can you ask God why he did this to me?" My mother hugged me very tightly, and my father left the room that night so I could sleep by her side. Every time I recall this moment, I feel the pain all over and start crying. People change, feelings dissipate, and promises break. But memories, and maybe even pains, will stay forever—I thought so at the time.

Enough was enough. I woke up one day and threw away all my medicine. I decided to finish my bachelor's degree, no matter what it took, and then go to Germany—my dream destination ever since I was a child. I finally finished my studies and was on my way there.

On my flight over to Germany, I felt pain all over my body. Nevertheless, I was confident that I made the right decision. I was reborn in Heidelberg even though life there was challenging at times. I remember taking the tram home one day, and I felt dizzy and began to sweat. My biggest fear was fainting in front of people, which is why I closed my eyes throughout the trip. When I heard the name of my train station being announced, I opened my eyes, left the tram, and slowly walked home. Once I got home, I laid on my bed and fell asleep. Lucky for me, the owner of the house where I resided was a medical doctor. And so began my treatment. It was quite expensive. So much so that I had to choose between dinner and lunch to budget for it. Money was not the problem; I knew I could ask my parents for it anytime. The problem was my ego. When I left Tunisia, I promised that I would solve every single one of my problems by myself.

The treatment worked, and my condition improved day by day. I was feeling much better and decided to continue my studies in Germany. The first semester was quite challenging because I did not fully recover, and I had to initially take an oral exam. Due to my condition, I was not well-prepared for it. After the exam, the professor told me: "I don't get it. How were you accepted here to study? Who do you think you are?" It was the first and only time I was humiliated in Germany for being a foreigner. The worst part was that it came from the mouth of a professor. Everything in my vision blackened at that moment. Facing humiliation in your home country because of your sickness was one thing. But being humiliated by a professor in a foreign country for no reason at all was too much. I felt miserable.

On my way home, I noticed the blooming cherry trees; it was springtime. But I felt the winter inside me. I found myself thinking: 'How often do people hurt you or stab you in the back?' My head would always picture the faces of these people. Every time I did, I felt a volcano inside my body, and my mind played sad music to make it more dramatic. Crazy! In such situations, people regret not instantly reacting and blame themselves for not expressing themselves properly at the time, even though it's too late to say, 'Please understand me!' I kept burning inside for days and months until I was utterly drained and did not even have the energy to wake up in the morning, let alone make my coffee, walk to the train, and carry on with my day. I kept procrastinating until I was afraid of the following morning's sun. So, I would go back to sleep until I woke up later, realizing another day was wasted. Then, I'd pretend that everything would be fine and look for excuses to escape the bitter truth that I was desperate to find a way out of this madness. Instead, I only tried to forget by watching endless political programs or spending hours on social media, telling myself to start again, fresh, the next day. Then, I woke up one day, balancing myself between disappointment and hopefulness. Suddenly, all my childhood complexes revealed themselves to me. I realized what people said—that you will forget everything with time—is a big lie. It all felt like a tornado, and I decided to further isolate and protect myself from others. This meant that I would enclose myself with my black thoughts. Mentally, this destroyed me. Physically, I didn't even want to leave my bed: neither for buying groceries, nor doing dishes (and the pile would just grow) nor for paying bills. I ignored everyone. I didn't even answer calls. I only answered days later, responding to their messages saying that I was busy. The worst part about all this was that I had already decided to lose from the beginning.

One day, my phone rang; it was a German colleague. I told her about what happened, so she proposed that we meet at the coordinator's office the very next day. We met and talked about everything in detail. They were very accommodating and constructed a plan that would enable me to continue my studies comfortably. The following week, I attended my professor's lecture despite what he had said to me. Surprisingly, he apologized to me at the end of the lecture. I felt a great sense of relief that day, and I did not hold a grudge against him like I did against the people from my bachelor-degree days in my home country. I realized something funny that day. My most painful experiences did not come from strangers but from the folks I was supposed to love and trust. Unfortunately, when I gave them more than they deserved, they gave back to me what I did not deserve. To such people, I say: "If you cannot be grateful, the least you can do is not be harmful." If I never blamed anyone or asked them for an apology, it doesn't mean what they did was right. My silence is not acceptance of what they did. Rather, it means that I chose to slam the door, move on, get over it, and continue my journey to success. Today, I can loudly say I succeeded.

Sometimes, things don't exactly go the way we'd like. We might say to ourselves that we're sick, tired, broke, tried too many times, or just unable to do something. But you know what? You are *not* what happened to you. You are what you choose to become. Are you not tired of playing the victim? Is it really worth your time worrying about the people who neither care for you nor deserve your attention? Basta!

To be successful is to continue despite difficulty and adversity, being emotionally detached, making mistakes and learning from them, and starting all over again. It's okay if you do something poorly, only as long as you realize there's a way to fix the problem and you put in the work to get up and start over. If the door is closed, jump in through the window. Feeling bad for not bettering yourself or not acting on your dreams is your choice. But keep this in mind: fear does not prevent death; it prevents life.

Some people will hurt you for no good reason. But there are also those who will recognize their errors, shed their ego, and apologize to you. Some will listen to you, lift you, protect you, and encourage you simply because they believe in you or like you. There are people you will only meet once, but they walk into your life at the right moment, add value to it, and remind you that you have a mission to fulfill and that you're amazing because you're different.

I remember the first time I went hiking in the mountains. I had a 2,000-meter peak to reach, and I was not wearing the appropriate clothing. Also, I was alone, and it was my first hiking experience. The higher I made it up the mountain, the colder and more dangerous it got. I was freezing, and I was scared. Even though I did not want to give up, I felt like I couldn't make it alone. Fortunately, I met two professional hikers, and I proposed to keep them company because I didn't want to meet with an accident in the more dangerous parts of the hike. They offered me hot tea, a pair of professional shoes, good company, and plenty of encouragement. These are the kind of people you rarely meet. They help you overcome your fears. They give you something even those closest to you do not offer, without seeking profit and without hesitation. All they want to do is simply help you at the right moment to reach your goal.

Every time I go through a difficult moment, I recall the story of the two hikers and the German colleague and coordinator. I tell myself that I can definitely reach my potential with the help of the right people, despite the many obstacles on the way. The most important thing is to start the journey to success. "I will either find a way, or make one," said Hannibal when he crossed the Alps with his elephants to invade Rome.[6] I know very well deep inside that if I truly desire something, the environment around me will find a simple way to make it happen. All I need to do is decide, start, and persevere.

Sometimes, we struggle with following the plan laid out for us, or we oppose what is termed "destiny." We get frustrated because things don't go the way we want. But behind these frustrations and difficulties are an abundance of blessings. We may not have the answer to "why?" at that moment, but we surely find out later when we realize the environment plans something better than we do. We can find meaning and learn from sickness, bankruptcy, toxic friendships, deception, and loss because, as Freud said, "Out of your vulnerabilities will come your strength."[7]

Life is filled with ups and downs, but isn't that how it's supposed to be? If we end up getting whatever we want, where's the meaning of living anymore? It's always important to be grateful to the universe and look at life from different perspectives.

I leave you with this. What if we lived our life as if we were reading a story? Would you want it to be a boring one or filled with action and fantasy? If you messed up, don't go back to the previous page. Keep reading your story, and keep the suspense going.

BIOGRAPHY

Emna Khechine is an interdisciplinary scientist based in Germany. She comes from Tunisia, the meeting point of several civilizations throughout history, which allows her to be open to all cultures and make friends with

---

6   Martin Svoboda, "Hannibal Quote #1863678," Quotepark.com, accessed July 8, 2021, https://quotepark.com/quotes/1863678-hannibal-i-will-either-find-a-way-or-make-one/.

7   "A Quote by Sigmund Freud," Goodreads (Goodreads), accessed July 8, 2021, https://www.goodreads.com/quotes/79982-out-of-your-vulnerabilities-will-come-your-strength.

people of different nationalities. Besides science, Emna is passionate about psychology and romance novels and has spent years reading books in four languages. She is dedicated to getting along with others, supporting them in their objectives, and finding the perfect solution for the people she cares about. She is also fiercely loyal to her values and will not follow others down a path that does not feel authentic. "Aut viam inveniam aut faciam" is her favorite Latin motto, meaning "Either I will find a way, or I will make one."

Connect with Emna Khechine via https://linktr.ee/emna.khechine

CHAPTER 13

Embrace The Grind

By Eric Diaz

I stood there in disbelief. I just couldn't believe two decades of hard work could come to this. I stood there, on the steps of the courthouse, watching as they auctioned our house away.

I still don't know why I was there. Maybe I wanted to punish myself. Maybe I hoped it wasn't true. Maybe I did it to motivate myself. Despite all that hard work it took to build what we had, here I was, in my early forties, and we just lost our house.

My parents divorced when I was nine. When my dad left, my mom kept my brother, and I was sent to live with my grandparents. I believed my grandmother when she told me I could grow up to become whatever I wanted to be. I didn't know I was a statistic.

She ingrained in me that what you do day after day would eventually pay off. Schooling was easy for me, so I did the work. Doing the work was not a problem. My grandmother saw to it that my homework was done before anything else. Playing outside and watching TV was secondary. Besides, I enjoyed the attention I'd get at every award ceremony because that's when my dad would usually show up.

In the eighth grade, I remember begging my grandmother to send me to a private high school. Both sides of my family went to the same public high school. Nothing wrong with that; I just wanted more. She cut me a deal. If every grade I received that year was an A, she would *think* about it. No problem.

When I brought home the final report card that year, I knew the moment I saw her face. The work I did was about to pay off. I didn't tell her that although I wanted to go to private school, it wasn't necessarily for academics. It was for football.

The year my parents split up was coincidentally the first year my dad signed me up for football. He took me to my first practice. As usual, my grandmother was the one who was tasked with taking me to practice every day after that. She took me every day, once my homework was done, of course, with no complaint. On the way home, we'd sometimes stop for ice cream on hot days.

I took to the game quickly once I realized I could hit people and channel the anger I held (against my parents' divorce) into something positive. Our team wasn't very good, but I fell in love with the game—the competition, the excitement of the games, and the cheering when I made a good play.

When I started high school, the social aspect was somewhat different, but school was school, and I handled it as usual. What challenged me was football. The year before I started, the team went undefeated, won the championship, and it seemed like every other kid my age decided to go there too. There were 113 guys on the freshman team! I had some work to do. A few weeks in, I got to travel to away games. But when I finally made the kickoff team, that was the crack in the door I needed to get in. I set a goal: to be a starter my senior year. That was it. It seems like so little in today's world, but back then, I was in one of the best schools around and surrounded by guys who could play.

When my senior year rolled around, I got what I wished for—well, at least what I personally wished for. I became a starter but realized that I should have set my eyes on a goal larger than myself. We lost three games that year, by a total of ten points. Not ten points a game, a total of ten points. One by two, another by three, and the other by five. Those ten points have a lot to do with who I am today. I have outworked people and poured into others to try to get those ten points.

After high school, I took a part-time job at night while enrolled in college and coached football at my old high school. Then, I found another job that almost stopped me from going to school. The money was just too good. Both of my grandfathers were first-generation born in the United States. So, while I was in college, I was never asked about school. I was always asked: "How is work?"

The second part-time job I had in college paid very well. Not just hourly, but five-figure bonuses at the end of each year. Having to pay my way through school, I decided to work full time. I switched to night school, not taking many classes in some semesters. But I never doubted that I would finish. In the past, and as I continue to get older, I realized it was a testament to who I am as a person. It took me nine years after I graduated high school to graduate with my first degree. It took me a while to realize it was something to be proud of; it's an example of perseverance. I was the first in my family to graduate from college.

My wife and I were married in 1996 and had our first of three sons that year. In 1998, I started law school. As a child, my grandmother asked me what I wanted to be when I grew up. I told her I wanted to be a lawyer. I've got to admit that I was quite proud of that accomplishment. With a lot of support, but no help from anyone but my wife, I worked my way through college and into law school.

The following year, we welcomed our second son and bought our first house. I was at a point in my life where I thought I could do no wrong. I had worked hard, made good money, and invested wisely. I was a self-made millionaire before I hit thirty.

Things were going so well that I decided to give back. I coached football at my old high school just to pour into young men—and to some who really needed it. I thought about becoming a full-time football coach, but I couldn't convince myself that it was the best thing for my family. You see, there are two kinds of coaches: those who *have* been fired and those who *will* be fired.

In 2002, we welcomed our third son into the world. The year after that, with some prodding from my wife, I quit my job, left law school behind me, and went to teach and coach at my alma mater. It was a considerable pay-cut, but I knew if I worked hard, it wouldn't matter. Everything would work out.

The following year, my first year of coaching, my wife's company was purchased, and she was asked to move out of state. Facing the loss of the second income stream, and after visiting the area, we decided to relocate. So, we moved to Texas, bought a home, and decided to start a new adventure.

My wife was a corporate executive, we were doing well, and I really wanted to coach football in Texas. So, I decided to go back to school, earn a degree in history and get my teaching credential.

As I was finishing up my degree, the opportunity to open my own business was presented. I was up for being my own boss, so I decided to take a leap of faith. I planned for everything, or so I thought. I found a location, bought equipment, and hired employees. All I had to do was what I always did: work hard every day.

What happened next, I would never have imagined: the economy tanked. My wife was let go. People stopped spending, which meant fewer sales for us. Why would they rely on a new business with a short track record? I saw no need to worry because I'd just keep working. Some days, I worked twenty hours. We pulled from our savings to invest more into the business. We pulled more to pay the mortgage. Then it ran out.

I thought I had planned for everything, but I was wrong. I planned for everything in my control.

There's a quote attributed to an anonymous NAVY seal: "Under pressure, you don't rise to the occasion, you sink to the level of your training."[8] I had the grit to overcome this because of how my grandmother raised me. I also owe it to my wife—the only woman besides my grandmother to completely believe in me.

---

8   "How the Navy SEALs Train for Leadership Excellence," Harvard Business Review, May 29, 2015, https://hbr.org/2015/05/how-the-navy-seals-train-for-leadership-excellence.

I'll be honest. There were times I felt like quitting. Permanently. But there was no way I would leave behind that type of pain as my legacy. I loved my wife too much, and my sons were watching. I wasn't going to walk out on them. Ever.

One of the reasons I have been successful is because I have the aptitude to learn. To pivot. To adjust. It's something I was forced to do my entire life. So why not use it to my advantage? I decided to focus on building relationships, not only with clients, but with others in the community. It was time to network and become a servant leader. I started with the game I love: football.

I started at a small private school that had just made the move from six-man football (I was unaware such a thing existed) to eleven-man. A few years later, I left for another private school in a higher division. The result: four State Championships in nine years.

Our business grew as we continued to serve. I served on the board of directors for two non-profits. Our business started to win awards: Business of the Month, the President's Award from the Chamber of Commerce, and Volunteer of the Year. So, we did what we felt we needed to do: diversify and open a few other businesses. Hard work pays off if you just stick with it.

One of my favorite poems is *Invictus* by William Ernest Henley. A line from that poem reads: "I am the master of my fate, I am the captain of my soul."[9] I firmly believe that if you do what needs to be done while adjusting to the circumstances you are dealt, you will become the master of your own fate.

---

9   William Ernest Henley, "Invictus by William Ernest Henley," Poetry Foundation (Poetry Foundation), accessed June 23, 2021, https://www. poetryfoundation.org/poems/51642/invictus.

BIOGRAPHY

Eric Diaz is a self-made entrepreneur who has built multiple successful businesses. He is also a four-time State Championship High School football coach in the state of Texas. Eric holds bachelor's degrees in Business Administration, History, and he attended Law School. Striving to be the ultimate servant leader and known for his grit, he is motivated by the Latin word "Invictus," meaning "Unconquerable." His mission is to lead by creating other leaders. He has been married to his wife Michele since 1996. Together, they have three sons: Thomas, Nicholas, and Jacob.

Connect with Eric Diaz via https://linktr.ee/ericdiaz

CHAPTER 14

Health: The Greatest Gift

By François Aubertin

"It is health that is real wealth and not pieces of gold and silver."[10]

—Mahatma Gandhi

"Dear God, I don't want to get like that when I am old!" I was eleven years old, and like a prayer, this thought haunted me during the twenty-minute drive home with my parents. I remained profoundly silent, mentally processing a surreal experience that had left me stunned. That day was my first time witnessing human sickness on such a scale. My only comparisons were my minor bruises and contusions from sports.

Late morning, on that warm summer day, my parents and I visited my grandfather at the nursing and rehabilitation center adjacent to the hospital where he had had a successful surgery for esophageal cancer. I still recall the thickness in the air as we entered the austere-looking building and the repulsive smell from bleach, urine, perspiration, and disinfectants.

We walked through the maze of corridors towards the ward where my grandpa was convalescing. Most of the rooms were occupied. I will never forget how many patients were painfully whining and groaning in their beds while others mumbled to themselves. Somehow, I must have

---

10 "Mahatma Gandhi Quotes," BrainyQuote (Xplore), accessed July 13, 2021, https://www.brainyquote.com/quotes/mahatma_gandhi_109078.

revealed my anguish as my mother softly told me that sometimes old people lose their mental faculties. Finally, we reached my grandpa's room.

My parents decided to go into grandpa's room first to make sure it was visually appropriate for me. They pointed to a sofa and told me to wait for their sign to come in. As I sat down, I noticed an elderly gentleman walking slowly while rolling an IV pole with a bag of fluid. He sat on the sofa across from me and smiled. I smiled back and nodded as a salutation.

No one is ever prepared when life throws something at you, especially at eleven years old. I had a feeling something very important was about to occur, and it did. The several minutes that followed were undoubtedly some of the most impactful in my life.

He engaged the conversation by saying, "Let me tell you why I'm here." The speed and tone he used in saying those few words made me pay attention, as though he was going to tell me a secret. He said he was there because of his sugar addiction. He loved Coca-Cola and used to drink three or four cans a day, sometimes more. He also enjoyed chocolate cakes and had desserts with every meal. I, too, loved desserts, so I listened attentively. He went on to say he had diabetes, and one of the effects of diabetes is reduced circulation to the extremities. He then explained he had undergone surgery on his foot to help his leg feel better. I looked down at the bandaged foot; it was shorter than his other foot despite the thickness of the bandage. I then realized his toes had been amputated. I remember chills running down my spine; I couldn't fathom how painful that must have been for him.

As he was finishing his story, another resident came and sat next to him. He was his roommate at the center. He was a big man recovering from heart surgery. His heart had stopped functioning and caused him extreme fatigue and discomfort. He confessed that he would have lived his life differently had he known the consequences of a poor diet.

Finally, my dad signaled me to come into my grandfather's room. I was relieved to go but, at the same time, unsettled about what I had just heard. I saluted the two gentlemen and proceeded to visit my grandpa.

"A sick man only wants one thing;
a healthy man wants a thousand things."[11]

—Confucius

That day was a wake-up call for me. I realized one thing: *health is the most precious commodity we have.* The candid stories of these two gentlemen touched me deeply and triggered a profound introspection into my existential self. Fearing a similar outcome, I committed to living a disease-free life after witnessing that some of these people would spend the last few weeks, months, or even years of their lives in a bed, in pain, or simply gone. For me, it was not living. I vowed that this would not be my reality—not that way and not in those conditions.

I was so motivated that I spent the rest of that day thinking of what I could do to prevent such ill outcomes. It was crystal clear in my mind: I would never want to be a patient in one of these centers. I vividly remember making a health pact to myself: "From now on, I will not drink sodas, avoid processed foods, and keep away from sugars." That day changed the trajectory of my life.

Fast forward to today, I am happy to report that I have followed what I had back then set to be my healthy lifestyle. I limited my sugar intake, made efforts to avoid processed foods altogether, and controlled my inherited skin condition, psoriasis. Of course, I cheated a few times, but I am where I need to be at fifty years old with my BMI (Body Mass Index). I don't require any medication, and my body feels like I'm in my twenties.

---

11   "'A Healthy Man Wants a Thousand Things...' - Confucius [1242x656]," OffBeat Quotes, April 6, 2020, https://offbeatquotes.com/a-healthy-man-wants-a-thousand-things-confucius-1242x656/.

"Health is the greatest gift, contentment the
greatest wealth, faithfulness the best relationship."[12]

—Buddha

Health is the greatest gift. I made it my mission to find, learn, and apply healthy life practices so I could help others avoid as much as possible any suffering or incapacitating health issues. Wouldn't you wish to maintain physical functionality, keep a sharp mind, and leave this plane of existence in a peaceful and honorable way, without regrets?

Setting my health vision at the age of eleven led me on a path of medical and paramedical studies. For thirty-one years, my passion has been to help people feel better through manual therapy. A few years ago, I branched out to expand my knowledge and expertise in a subtler field: nutrition and metabolic health. Subtler because, contrary to structural issues, which can be resolved sometimes in one or a few sessions, metabolic health may require more time before yielding observable results. The reward, though, is quite satisfying.

Let's face it: health problems are on the rise. More and more people are struck with diseases at a younger age than previous generations. In the last sixty years, we have seen a constant increase of chronic illnesses: heart and lung diseases, strokes, Alzheimer's, arthritis, and diabetes, to name only a few.

Fortunately, there are many holistic approaches to health restoration and ways to stay healthy for as long as possible. Scientific discoveries are bringing to light what our bodies really need to function better and longer. There are no miracle pills or supplements yet. When sickness strikes, the journey to remission often requires time, courage, motivation, discipline, determination, and hope.

---

12 "Buddha Quotes," BrainyQuote (Xplore), accessed July 13, 2021, https://www. brainyquote.com/quotes/buddha_140966.

"The doctor of the future will give no medicine, but will instruct his patients in care of the human frame, in diet, and in the cause and prevention of disease."[13]

—Thomas Edison

I personally believe in going back to the basics: proper diet, breathing and movement, and a positive mindset. Many holistic practitioners share this approach. It promotes lifestyle changes to remedy or prevent the onset of diseases altogether rather than cure them. In my experience, I have seen spectacular recoveries when people adopted a healthy and holistic approach to their health.

Where do we start when we are sick? When we are first informed of an illness, the usual reactions are panic or paralysis. It is quite normal in the face of the unknown. Below is my four-step approach to address a health issue or any important situation coming your way.

When you face a difficulty or challenge, just like an obstacle on the road, the first reflex should be to **slow down**. Slowing down allows you to reduce the distractions around the problem that need to be solved. The next step is to **assess the situation**: look for and evaluate possible options. The third step is to **elaborate on a plan**: proceed with the most logical option to maneuver around the obstacle. If plan "A" does not work, go to plan "B," and so forth. Once you've successfully overcome the obstacle, you may **resume** the route to your destination, knowing that you have learned one more problem-solving lesson, which is now part of your toolbox.

When it comes to health, the steps are similar. If the problem is very complex, though, an expert's help may be necessary to assess the situation,

---

13 Chester Buckenmaier, "'The Doctor of the Future Will Give No Medication but Will Interest His Patients in the Care of the Human Frame, Diet and in the Cause and Prevention of Disease'-Thomas A. Edison (1847-1931)," U.S. Medicine, April 11, 2020, https://www.usmedicine.com/editor-in-chief/the-doctor-of-the-future-will-give/.

determine the best options, and elaborate on a strategic plan to solve the issue.

The more important the health issue, the more it is necessary to **slow down**. Take some deep breaths! Most people omit this simple action during stressful situations. A deep breath connects you to your present mind, being here and now. Oxygen helps you think more clearly. When you are in the present moment, you can focus your attention on what matters the most—in this case, your health. I strongly suggest learning some breathing techniques as they are proven to regulate the autonomic nervous system, promote relaxation, alkalize the body, and lower cortisol levels—all good things in times of crisis.

Backtracking and reflecting on how we got here can be a way to **assess the situation**. This important step requires your full attention. Distractions prevent you from focusing on your objectives as they use your time and energy elsewhere. Removing the clutter and simplifying your life can greatly enhance finding solutions and reaching your goals. Multitasking is not efficient, no matter what you think about it.

Elaborate on a plan. The plan will differ depending on the health challenge you want to address. In my experience, no matter what the health issue may be, diet remains the most important factor to positively influence the outcome.

"Let food be thy medicine and medicine be thy food."[14]

—Hippocrates

You heard it before: "We are what we eat!" You, and only you, have full control of your diet. You wouldn't put diesel in a Ferrari. Why would you put the wrong foods in your body? Start giving it the best and most nutritious foods available to you. Your body will love you and run more smoothly.

---

14 "A Quote by Hippocrates," Goodreads (Goodreads), accessed July 13, 2021, https://www.goodreads.com/quotes/62262-let-food-be-thy-medicine-and-medicine-be-thy-food.

A cleaner diet will reduce the three main causes linked to ninety percent of today's health challenges: chronic inflammation, type B malnutrition, and dysbiosis (gut microbiota imbalance). It will provide a healthier cellular matrix or superior metabolic health. This is the first step in assisting our cells in rejuvenation.

Our bodies were designed to move—every single day. Our modern lifestyle has considerably diminished our physical activities. Find a partner and get going! There are many fun activities to share with friends, such as cycling, walking, jogging, Pilates, tennis, yoga, etc. Maybe simple chair exercises are the only thing you may be able to muster right now. The goal is to practice movement daily and activate circulation.

> "Our greatest glory is not in never falling,
> but in rising every time we fall."[15]
>
> —Confucius

There is no clear path or straight line towards health. We win some battles and lose others; accidents may happen along the way, and genetic factors may also play a role. However, no matter what happens, having a positive mindset helps minimize any fallouts. When plan "A" fails, go to plan "B." Never give up. Life is full of miracles and surprises, and wonders never cease to happen.

> "Divide each difficulty into as many parts as is feasible
> and necessary to resolve it, and watch the whole transform."[16]
> —Rene Descartes

Slow down and breathe. Set your goals using a step-by-step strategy. This is the best way to keep your motivation intact while progressing towards

---

15   "Confucius Quotes," BrainyQuote (Xplore), accessed July 13, 2021, https://www.brainyquote.com/quotes/confucius_101164.

16   Kiersten M., "Inspirational Quotes," Wonder, November 2, 2019, https://start.askwonder.com/insights/inspirational-quotes-kun5qndhb.

your desired reality. Instead of setting a single, herculean goal, divide the course into a series of smaller goals. You will still go in the direction of your main goal but will win many smaller and easier battles along the way. This strategy helps you stay motivated, rewards you with each victory, and builds your momentum towards your ultimate goal. A huge goal may be too hard to conquer at once and cause you to lose concentration and confidence.

I am sharing how I became passionate about health and healing at a young age because I care and strongly believe that no one should suffer unnecessarily. Nobody has to walk this journey alone. I'd like to offer my help and share my knowledge and skills with others open to holistic approaches. We often take health for granted. Let's not wait to be faced with an issue to become proactive. I believe everyone can enjoy life to its fullest, age gracefully, and keep all their faculties until the end. Start today by taking positive actions to design the way you want your future to be.

To your health!

BIOGRAPHY

François Aubertin is a Canadian health practitioner, teacher, and speaker in the fields of manual therapy and holistic health. He holds a Canadian Diploma in Osteopathy and a master's degree in science from the University of Québec at Montréal. For more than thirty years, François has successfully helped people resolve physical and nutritional health challenges. He has worked in many countries, including Canada, the UK, France, Central and South America, and the United States of America. He had the privilege of working with athletes from Cirque du Soleil and, more recently, remedying US Navy Seals. François is an active member of the Osteopathic European Academic Network (OsEAN), where he enjoys sharing new healing concepts with his peers and keeping up to date with science. His passion is to help as many people as possible reach their optimal health. You may learn more about his services at francoisaubertin. com/

Connect with François Aubertin via linktr.ee/francoisaubertin

CHAPTER 15

The Difficult Sacrifices That Changed My Life

By Gliza Gail Mangibong

All the sacrifices and choices you've made your entire life: were they worth it? Why so? And why do I pose this question to you? Because I know every single one of us has made a sacrifice, or rather, many sacrifices.

Every decision we make has corresponding sacrifices. We definitely cannot make them all in one sitting, but we do prioritize the ones that matter most. In the process of prioritizing, we give up one thing in exchange for the other.

When it comes to achieving our dreams and goals, we tend to suppress them because of our responsibilities. However, we don't realize that we sometimes need to achieve our goals to fulfill our responsibilities. Due to this aforementioned misconception, some people stop chasing their dreams or only do the bare minimum. They neither move further nor soar higher—perhaps because they are comfortable where they are. On the other hand, some soar high as they try to fulfill their responsibilities, that they detract themselves from those said responsibilities by too intense of a focus on their dreams. Such people need to realize that their responsibilities serve as stepping stones toward their goals. Whatever be the reason, every individual has their "why."

Now, while working on our goals, we will most likely experience difficulties, trials, and hardships. These fall under two categories: human-made and a result of our environment. The former trials are the ones we create for ourselves. The latter comes from our living environment, workplace, or any other environment in which we find ourselves. During the process of undergoing difficulties, we sacrifice our time, some of our other goals, and even our very selves.

What we truly want and the reasons for pursuing it can simply be answered by the question: Why? *Why* did you sacrifice your time? *Why* did you sacrifice your dream? *Why* did you sacrifice yourself? *Why* did you make that choice? *Why* did you give up something valuable in exchange for something worth less?

Given all that I have been through and where I am now, I feel free and happy. Those who know what it is to be truly successful can see it, but others may not because their idea of being successful is limited to financial stability. Unfortunately, people still tend to treat this as a hard and fast rule. Not everyone who is financially stable is free and happy. My point is that being successful is a subjective experience based on an individual's perception.

It has been years since I've grown up in a negative environment. It got to the point where I was unable to know right from wrong. Living according to the expectations of other people was like being a hawk trapped inside a cage. It cannot do anything; it does not have a voice. It cannot decide for itself. People in such situations always consult others before making decisions. They end up sacrificing themselves to the extent that they neglect (and even forget) what makes *them* comfortable and happy. Like the hawk, they wish to spread their wings, given a chance. Sadly, they are restricted by many limitations.

Since my childhood, I was made to live up to others' expectations, and I was even compared to others. I had to play copycat so that I could mimic those who appreciated and pleased the status quo. Even if I were to do something that was truly an accomplishment in itself, if it were seen as a mistake or against the expected standards, it would not be appreciated. Doing nothing also got people to spill hurtful words that cut right into my heart. In order to feel "belonged," I had to conform to the standards of right and wrong according to my peers.

If I tried to stand up on my feet, I would be dragged down most of the time. This happened so many times that I was unsure of what exactly I wanted to do, thinking that if I just went with the flow of what everyone else wanted, all would pass by and set itself in place. After a year, nothing changed. Any decision I tried to make always produced an opponent. Even worse than battling such an opponent was having to deal with hearsay, gossip, and rumors about myself. Doing the "right" thing brought on a negative reaction. Doing the wrong thing would make it worse.

I wondered about freedom. I wanted out of this cage. I began to foresee myself on top of a mountain, taking in this beautiful scenery: the scent of the trees, the wind blowing all my worries and problems away, and the birds chirping their sweet music into my ears. Picturing this, I realized: "IT'S MY LIFE! I'M IN CONTROL!!!"

But fully internalizing this thought would take a lengthy process of acceptance, courage, change of mindset, and adaptability. This would be the "fuel" that would keep pushing me forward no matter what would happen. This mindset was the last straw of hope—of which I would *not* let go.

First, I needed acceptance. Yes, you read that right—*acceptance*. I needed to accept that living in this world, I could not please everybody. There would always be people who would judge me from the little information they have or simply without any basis. A person will judge you based on their situation, whether or not you are doing the right thing. Why should you not care about them? So that you don't hurt yourself. You can really minimize the hurt of what others think and say about you if you carry that mindset—especially when people gossip or are against you.

Next, I needed courage. Courage is what makes me worthy of respect because I act rightly in the face of discouragement (in my case, my moral or mental health).

Following this, I needed a change of mindset—from wrong to right. Allow me to elucidate. Mindset is your state of mind or manner of thinking that is affected by your environment and life experience. Having the right mindset brings in positive energy. That being said, I needed to sustain any positive vibe to keep me going and from falling back down time and again. I needed to set my mind with positive vibes to not be depressed or negatively affected by my surrounding environment.

Lastly, I needed adaptability. Adaptability is the ability to adjust to various conditions. In the context of pushing against those who oppose you, adaptability is not so much contradicting their opinions as much as it is finding a way to counteract their opinions. This is so they can see that you are not completely wrong, and they are not completely right (a sort of reverse psychology approach, in a way). Once I learned to do this, I was able to start standing up for myself.

In order to make a drastic change in my life, I needed to take the initial step. That first step can have a tremendous impact on your life. It did for me because it allowed me to break out of my comfort zone. Nothing would have happened if I stood where I was. I would have remained in someone else's shadow and not find my true self. I needed to first appreciate and love myself for the good and bad within me. Only then would I be able to know my strengths and weaknesses.

Further, I had to turn my weaknesses into strengths. Otherwise, they would only serve to pull me down and stop me in my tracks. To do this, I needed to give up certain things; I had to sacrifice all my time spent thus far and start over again. Knowing that I was going to lose something in the process empowered me to continue what I started, and it gave me the strength to go on so that all I sacrificed would have been worth it.

Despite all the good and bad things I heard about myself, I self-reflected and realized that I was neither stepping on others' dignity nor doing something against society. Once I came to this realization, I was able to continue pursuing my dreams and goals. Only this time, I would pursue them along with people who were authentic and supportive of me to the end. And these are the kind of people I would stick with because they had the ability to uplift me and help me reach what I aim for. On the same note, I distanced myself from those who wanted to pull me down because they were the reason why I was unable to move forward when I wanted to. All their negative words and comments, gossiping, and hearsay about me—I had taken it all in. More times than not, I almost became rebellious (in the negative sense). But my nature did not allow that to happen because I'm an overthinker. I thought about the negativity that a bad, rebellious nature could bring about. Having analyzed the pros and cons, I realized that acting in such a manner would have dragged me down to the pit. Instead, I cried to relieve my burden, after which I would say: "I will prove them wrong! I am not that kind of person, and I *will not* become the person they think I am!" I took their slander as a challenge and channeled it into becoming the person I am today. I took what was negative and used it to my advantage, and I became the opposite of my naysayers' image of me.

Going back to what I said earlier, I made many sacrifices to get where I am because I was absolutely certain of what I wanted to achieve. I continued to soar higher even though many tried to pull me down. I was stubborn (in the good sense of the word) and only soared higher and higher until those who were pulling me down could not keep up with me. Like an eagle, I did not resist my flight to the skies; I only kept going until they gave up. Like an eagle flying in the storm, I did not give up but only kept flying until I found a place to perch until the storm passed.

It was a new beginning for me. I realized that life had no limits to those who wanted to spread their wings. But *what* exactly made my new life what it is today? All the difficulties, trials, and hardships I had to go through. Instead of letting them bring me down, I turned them into lessons, challenges, and steppingstones to reach my dreams and goals. I am who I am today because of every challenge I went through. Had it not been for those challenges, perhaps I would have developed a different perspective, view of life, and mode of thinking. What I went through molded and built me to become someone—a better version of my former self.

To answer your question: yes, my choices and sacrifices were all worth it. It is because of the same choices and sacrifices that I broke out of my comfort zone, let myself be molded, have the best brought out of me, and used all my weaknesses as strengths, which ultimately allowed me to become a better version of myself. Although it took some time to get where I wanted to be, and even though I sometimes think about what I missed out on in my past years, what is most important is that I am now here: living without worrying about what others think of me and making decisions with my freewill, not catering to the opinions of others.

At this point, nothing can hold me back (even if I wanted it to). Life is too short, and not everyone has the chance to live it to its fullest. If you've achieved such happiness in life, then you have met Ayn Rand's definition of the word: "Happiness is the state of consciousness which proceeds from the achievement of one's values."[17]

People see the real me when I spread my wings fully. Hopefully, they come to understand that they should neither prejudge someone without any basis nor drag them down.

Know that happiness is life's fulfillment. Only then will you know you have no boundaries.

BIOGRAPHY

Gliza Gail Mangibong is known for being a life changer, challenger, and survivor. Knowing how tough life can be, she stands her ground to prove her value and worth. She is motivated by the proverb: "A journey of a thousand miles begins with a single step."

Connect with Gliza Gail Mangibong via https://linktr.ee/glizagail05

---

17 "Happiness Is the State of Consciousness," ReDirections Career Life Solutions, July 23, 2014, https://www.careerlifesolutions.com/happiness-is-the-state-of-consciousness/.

CHAPTER 16

Goal Setting

By Grace Kansiime

The year 2020 started out with much excitement, and most of us claimed it as the year of success and fulfilled dreams! Not being any different for me, I started 2020 feeling love and joy from both family and friends, and I focused on the goals I set! I could not ask for more; it was perfect! I made my usual beginning-of-the-year declarations, and I was ready to go.

Soon after this, the pandemic unexpectedly took over the world! Like many people, I was devastated. You see, at the time of the pandemic, I was more than 10,000 km away from home, but this was not my biggest problem. The pandemic struck right around the time I was supposed to return home. I was close to completing my one-year training and eagerly waiting to return home.

Working in a hospital and being at risk of contracting the virus every day did not help me feel better. Every time I walked into the hospital, I couldn't help but wonder if I walked out with the virus!

Then, the whole world almost came to a standstill with no flights! I lost count of the number of times I had to reschedule my flight. Being so far away from my loved ones made me feel lost and trapped.

While searching for a way out, I took a break to think, to reconnect, and it was during this time I counted my blessings despite the prevailing challenges.

I had my family and friends. Thankfully, the pandemic in my country was not too bad at the time, and my loved ones were safe. I was completing my one-year training despite the pandemic. This was a great achievement, and so I started thinking about the journey that led me here.

You have most likely seen many people become doctors, so you won't understand why this is beyond success for me. I will therefore give you some perspective.

I come from Uganda, a small country in East Africa, and until recently, society and culture would treasure a male child more than a girl child. At the time, my parents were ridiculed for having only girls and were considered obnoxious because they wanted to educate us—girls!!

Recently I asked my friends on Facebook what they wanted to become when they were children, and I got all sorts of answers, as you can imagine. It was fun to see how far some of my friends diverted from their childhood dreams, but then, that's life, right? Do you ever ask yourself: what shapes our childhood dreams into reality? What we become or achieve later in life is shaped by our experiences, external influences, modelling, and our childhood (I will talk more about this later).

Most of us wanted to be like our parents, their friends, or at least someone we knew very early in childhood. These are the people with whom we spent most of our time. We aspired to be teachers because of how our teachers impacted us, nurses because of our mothers, policemen because they were smart, or superman because he saved the world! Notice how all this came from the people around us; this is the beginning of how the world influences us.

As we grow up and become influenced by society, we believe stories told to us. These are stories about us or our life's events, and all these stories shape who we become.

Growing up, my parents were small-scale farmers. Neither of them had a college degree, so they worked hard to fend for us. The only professionals I knew were my teachers, and at the time, we had no TV, so there were no inspiring TV characters either. All I remember was my parents telling me to study hard and become more successful than them.

But what was I to become? As we grow older, we understand that goals are only attained after they are set! They must be specific and time-bound. My goal as a child was to "just be better than what my parents were!" Whether this meant affording a few nice things that they couldn't afford or have a better house than they did, I don't know. Notice that though I was determined to become better than my parents, I had neither first-hand experience of someone who was better nor inspiring enough for me to emulate. This went on until I completed elementary school.

My journey towards my real dreams began with two new teachers who joined my school during my final elementary school year (or primary seven, as we call it here in Uganda). These two were young and smart, and they spoke to us in English at all times! They were more inspiring than my other teachers. One day, they asked everyone in the class what we wanted to become when we grew up. All I wanted was to be 'better than my parents,' nothing specific. "You should become a doctor," said one of the two teachers who, to me, knew all the English and mathematics in the world! His colleague agreed. They did not realise what they had just done! They sparked something within me. I now had a goal, and I couldn't wait to get home and tell my parents! That school day must have felt longer than usual.

I ran ahead of everyone home and went straight to my dad and, with so much excitement, told him I wanted to become a doctor; that was how I greeted my parents that evening.

My dad looked at me and responded, "I will do all it takes to make you a doctor as long as you do what it takes—get the marks." What my dad meant was that if I got the grades, he would strive to obtain the money to get me into a good high school. Hmm, I had not thought about this. This was the first and most important lesson from my parents: I was responsible for my success. I had to do my part. And so, the long journey began.

Every journey has its hills and valleys, and mine was no different. I have had my failures, but I never quit. Towards the end of my lower secondary level (high school) exams, I scored my best grades in non-science subjects. This meant I would study these during my advanced secondary level (A-level). In our education system, A-level is when you really start defining your career path. I got into the school of my choice, but I could only select non-science subjects based on my grades. This meant never becoming a doctor.

My dad picked my admission letter for me, but he did something that very few parents would do. He insisted that I become a doctor and go for the sciences. In my absence, he signed an agreement with the headteacher, on my behalf, that if I didn't score a specific grade at the end of the first term, I would be expelled for poor performance! Lesson number two from my dad: **trust**, **commitment**, and **hard work**. He had taken this to another level. He proved that he trusted my abilities, and this motivated me even further. He committed on my behalf, so I had to put in the hard work. That was the only way. That was my defining moment. I still had the opportunity to study my original non-science subjects, but I decided to follow my dream.

I have recently learnt from one of my mentors the meaning of the word 'DECIDE.' 'CIDE,' as in de**cide**, sui**cide**, and geno**cide** means 'to kill.' When you decide, you kill off all other options. And, with only one option, you FOCUS, i.e., **F**ollow **O**ne **C**ourse **U**ntil **S**uccessful.

My biggest failure. In my country's education system, the moment of truth is when you get your A-level final exams result. This determines your university/career course. My biggest failure: I could not study medicine in university since I was below the cut-off grade. My dream was fast-crushing before my eyes. All the hard work had gone to waste! I was very disappointed, and I couldn't stop blaming myself. I was responsible for my failure here. My parents had kept their end of the bargain and got me into my choice school. None of my teachers missed a class or failed to give me time, so it was me!

Plans change, decisions don't. With a bit of research, I learnt I could obtain a medical-related diploma and later join medical school. Talk about second chances! If you are heading north toward your goals and you hit a roadblock, you don't quit. You can turn east or west and eventually still get to your goal. Change the plan or route to your goal, but never quit.

Never waste a second chance. Even worse, don't fail to recognize it. Second chances mostly present themselves in our lowest moments, and we become focused on our failures/losses that we miss them. They last only a few seconds sometimes.

God helped me to recognize my second chance, and I grabbed it. My life depended on it. While in school, I was more committed and worked harder. My friends didn't understand why I worked so hard. For me, it was not just getting through the diploma, finding a job, and living my life. This was just a stepping stone, but I had to excel to get into medical school. There was no room for failure. I had no weekends off and limited holidays during those three years.

I now know that when you want something so badly, the universe will conspire to give it to you against all odds! Never forget this.

Be very careful who you associate with. In life, most people won't get it; don't waste your time on them. Unfortunately, sometimes, it's your family and friends but strangers too. They won't understand why you work hard or why you want it so bad. It is easier to pass by and ignore the opinions of strangers. But what of those close to us? We think they know us well enough that we allow their opinions to define us. But no, my friend, you have a choice to believe what they say about you. Choose your company carefully. Love your family, but choose your friends and beliefs. Those friends who always think you can't or won't, those who always drain your positive energy, and those who always feed you with negativity, please run away from them.

Remember, if you take in positivity, it's what you retain and pass on to others. The inverse is also true. Look at the people in your circle and ask yourself if they support or discourage your dreams. I have met many from both categories. I am not saying ditch your family and friends, but understand this and know how to protect yourself and your dreams.

I finally got into medical school after my diploma and achieved my dream. Then, it hit me, 'What next?' Luckily, as you go through undergraduate training, you realise there's postgraduate which one starts planning by default, followed by a fellowship or PhD. And the quest goes on as one wishes.

But what about in life, when you set a goal and achieve it? What next? This question should be answered much before you achieve your set goal. Like life, setting goals and achieving or modifying them is a journey. And just like a journey, you don't get to the next checkpoint to decide what next; you decide along the way. So set goals, review them, set more goals, and achieve them while setting others along the way. Always move towards a set goal; otherwise, you will stagnate.

I have completed my medical degree and gone on to do my postgraduate. As most people were cursing 2020 because of the pandemic, I accomplished yet another achievement: my nephrology fellowship training!

I am not saying that goals are easy to achieve, and I'm not promising you constant success, but you will only achieve what you set out to! If you want to be lucky, remember what Thomas Jefferson said: "I find that the harder I work, the more luck I seem to have."[18]

Opportunities will only come to those who are prepared to take them. **Set your goals and never quit on yourself.** As the pandemic rages on, we still live, set new goals, and achieve them; that's why life is beautiful. It goes on and on. As Conrad Hilton said: "Success seems to be connected with action. Successful people keep moving. They make mistakes, but they don't quit."[19]

---

18 "A Quote by Thomas Jefferson," Goodreads (Goodreads), accessed April 14, 2021, https://www.goodreads.com/quotes/693932-i-find-that-the-harder-i-work-the-more-luck.

19 Tony Lynch, "Success Seems to Be Connected with Action.," Keep Thinking Big, January 20, 2014, https://keepthinkingbig.com/success-seems-connected-action/.

BIOGRAPHY

Grace Kansiime is a medical doctor and kidney-diseases specialist, currently teaching medical students at Mbarara University of Science and Technology. From humble beginnings in Uganda, Grace continues to rise and inspire young people. She is always willing to help others achieve their full potential. Her favourite quote about success is by Winston Churchill: "Success is not final; failure is not fatal: It is the courage to continue that counts." She is married to Pliers, since 2014. They are blessed with a daughter, Mariah, and two sons, Franco and Michael.

Connect with Grace Kansiime via https://linktr.ee/gkansiime

CHAPTER 17

Unlock The Power Within You . . . It's There

By Helen Martin

Every one of us is born for greatness. However, the unfortunate truth is that most of the human population will never find it. There are many reasons for that. One of those reasons is that most of our belief systems, behaviours, and habits are formed by the age of seven. Whether they are beneficial to us or not, we spend the rest of our lives with those habits, proving those beliefs and behaviours to be right.

So, there lies a massive dilemma for those who've had negative experiences as a child. You'll spend the rest of your life continuing your bad habits and proving your negative beliefs and behaviours right, unless you change your thoughts and, by extension, your actions.

There's no question that my experiences as a child have moulded the person I am today. No girl should grow up without their mum, but that was my reality.

My mum was diagnosed with breast cancer when I was ten. I didn't ever think she would die until I secretly read my sister's diary and saw that she wrote, '*My auntie told me today that mum was going to die.*' It hit me like a tonne of bricks, and life was never the same after that. Unfortunately, the inevitable happened, and after years of battling breast cancer, my mum passed away when I was fourteen.

In the years that followed, other family members passed away, and close relationships broke down. It was a continuous feeling of loss, and my walls went up to protect myself. I became fiercely independent—washing, cooking, cleaning, organising myself, school, working, helping my dad support my sister and me, and making decisions most young girls didn't have to.

That fierce independence within me helped me develop 'grit.' Still, it led to relationship issues, pushing away friends for my career, self-doubt, lack of self-belief, exhaustion, and illness. The 'grit' helped me push through full-time work and study. I gained qualifications in accounting, a Bachelor of Business in Marketing, and then went on to pursue a law degree.

While working full-time and halfway through my law degree, life threw me a curveball. I contracted a virus called Guillain-Barre. Within three days, I couldn't move my arms above my head or walk properly. Thankfully, I didn't know, at the time, that this virus could kill you.

The simplest tasks became impossible. I could no longer wash my hair, get dressed, let alone walk very far. I was in my late twenties and incredibly scared. It should have been exciting times. I was young and had been promoted to Executive Director at work. I had just bought my first home, and my partner and I had moved in together. However, within three days, I went from being on top of the world to not being able to work, not being able to walk, and not being able to enjoy the simple joys of socialising with my friends and partner. After finally getting over losing my mum, life spiralled downward again.

It was a very lonely time in my life. I had to dig deep and find the strength I didn't know I had. I thought all my goals and dreams were fading away. I spent six months going to the hospital every day, doing hydrotherapy to get my arms and legs moving again. I lost touch with my friends, and I couldn't do things normal people do. My partner supported me throughout my journey, but I had no idea how much he was struggling. He wanted to support me, but he also wanted to live his life as a young man in his twenties.

When I finally got better, my partner left our relationship. Heartbreak, all over again. It just seemed like blow after blow. Here I was, losing someone I loved once more. How many more times was this going to happen? All my fears and insecurities were heightened once more. Although it was devastating at the time, the breakup needed to happen because that partner is now my husband. We love each other dearly, and we have two amazing boys only fourteen months apart.

What a roller coaster, but hey, that's life. There's always something that will come up to challenge our strength, beliefs, and mental toughness. What I realised over time is that my outer world is a direct reflection of my inner world—meaning, my thoughts. We can either let the circumstances around us rule our lives, or we can take control by mastering our thoughts. At the end of the day, it doesn't matter what's happening to us, it's the way we think about it.

You get to choose whether your life controls you or you control it. You can choose to worry, stress, and play the victim, or you can choose to accept what is (I didn't say you have to like it) and focus your energy on finding solutions instead of wasting your energy on the problems.

The best thing I've learned to do during challenging times is moving out of my 'emotions' and into 'evaluation.' I give myself up to twenty-four hours to feel whatever I need to feel, and then pick myself up, put my big girl pants on, and evaluate the situation so I can focus on finding effective solutions for whatever I am dealing with.

You can use this strategy in all areas of your life—relationships, business, friendships, your children, anything. Feel what you need to feel: this could be anger, sadness, hurt, tears, grief, frustration, being overwhelmed, etc. But a maximum of twenty-four hours later, move on from your internal emotions and evaluate the situation externally. Shift your focus. It is only when you do this that you can find rational solutions to your situation. There is absolutely no benefit to being stuck in your emotions. It only holds you back.

Through challenging situations in my life—and yes, there are more to come—learning to get out of my emotions into evaluation helps me through anything.

Unfortunately, the losses of family members continued. This time, it was on my husband's side. His mum passed away due to cancer, and only a few years later, while his dad was playing tennis on a Saturday afternoon, he dropped to the ground due to a heart attack and never recovered.

Life took us on a completely different path after that. At the time, my career was going well. I was General Manager of an association where I had worked for sixteen years. My husband, Paul, had his own business, and the boys were transitioning to school. I guess you could say life was settled and predictable. But we had a massive decision to make. There were so many things to deal with regarding Paul's father's estate. We had to decide to either stay in the city and deal with the situation remotely or pick up our life and move to the country to take care of everything.

The decision was easy for my husband, but I was torn. I liked my comfort zone, job, stable salary, and the predictability of our life. I finally had stability back in my life with my family, career, and health. What would I do if I resigned from my job and left the corporate world? How would I replace my general manager's salary? How would I help support my family financially?

In the end, we decided to go. I reluctantly resigned from my job, and we moved to the country.

Fear was in full force, and all the insecurities were back again. However, when one door closes, another one opens.

I changed careers and never went back into the workforce. I explored this big wide world of being an entrepreneur. Once I let myself relax with my newfound freedom, I realised that I didn't want to go back into the corporate world. I went from wearing suits every day to whatever I wanted. I was suddenly in control of my every move. I was able to drop the boys off and pick them up from school every day. I could finally do all the things the corporate world had constrained me from doing as a mum.

It was really stressful leaving my career and making such a massive change. But it was ultimately my choice. Everything in our life requires choices. We are in control. Although scary, I consciously chose to get off the nine-to-five hamster wheel, and it's been an incredible ride ever since.

Fast forward seven years, I have now become a multiple six-figure earner in the online world. I am building my own brand and teaching home-based business owners how to bring their businesses online. I have my own branding course and coaching community, and I'm a certified mentor for an American mentorship company. I'm a network and affiliate marketer, and I still do consulting accounting work and teach classes at the local gym just for fun. First and foremost, though, I'm a mum, wife, daughter, and sister.

Being an entrepreneur is quite challenging. It would have been easier getting another job. I had absolutely no experience with online marketing or building businesses online, but I desired to learn. I knew if I wanted an outcome different from the nine-to-five grind, I had to get uncomfortable and just fail forward with something new. There's no question that if you want something more for your life, you must be willing to get uncomfortable.

Over the years, I have learned to take control of my life with my thoughts. I became very aware that our brain is designed to keep us safe, and its natural instinct is to talk me out of doing things that make me uncomfortable. No matter what the situation is—whether it's exercising, eating healthy, starting a new business, approaching someone about your business—if it's slightly scary or difficult, your brain is designed to talk you out of it to keep you safe and comfortable.

So, when you're scared to do something, remind yourself what your brain is designed to do and consciously push past the thoughts that stop you. Feel the fear and do it anyway.

My journey has had its challenges, but some people are worse off and still happy. A trip to Manilla reminded me of this. My entrepreneurial journey has taken me to many places overseas, and one of those was Manilla, where I had the opportunity to help feed hundreds of underprivileged children. There was this one little boy who gravitated to me as soon as we got there. He saw how hot and sweaty I was. It was scorching hot. He ran off, found a piece of cardboard, and didn't leave my side all day, fanning me with his piece of cardboard to help me cool down.

What struck me was how happy these children were, yet they had nothing. I learned a valuable lesson that day. You don't need anything to be happy other than your own thoughts. It's all about your perception of life. It's the same in business. Your beliefs, happiness, success, and ability to move quickly from problems to solutions are all up to you.

Love yourself enough to be the person you know you can be. Step into that person now. Don't wait for it to happen. Don't wait for the approval of others. Just make it happen, no matter how scary or uncomfortable it is. I went from knowing nothing about the online world to become a multiple six-figure earner in a relatively short period. No one else made that happen but me.

If it is to be, it is up to me. That has certainly been the case in my life despite what it throws my way. Remember, it's not the circumstances happening around you that are important. It's how you *think* about those circumstances and how quickly you shift your energy from your problems to solutions.

Control your thoughts and explore your greatness. It's yours for the taking.

BIOGRAPHY

Helen Martin is a social media coach, speaker, and author. She also has an e-commerce business and is the founder of her 'Online Crew' brand. With a Bachelor of Business in Marketing, most of Helen's working life was in the corporate world. However, in her early forties, she reluctantly resigned from her general manager's role due to family circumstances. Ultimately, this pivot in Helen's life led her to explore how to build businesses online, and now, she is a multiple six-figure online entrepreneur. Her passion is to empower home-based business owners, propel their business online, build their brand, and achieve the success they desire. Helen resides in Australia with her husband and two boys.

Connect with Helen Martin via https://linktr.ee/helenmartinonline

CHAPTER 18

Beyond Success

By Isabella Kibunri

"If you are not willing to be a fool, you can't become a master."[20]

—Jordan Peterson

Waiting for a long time to do what you love is wrong. There is no "right time." When an opportunity comes our way, we often leave it aside, thinking it is the worst thing ever to happen. But when we realize that we missed it, then regret kicks in. One thing I have realized about success is that you have to start whenever something comes into your mind. If it's something that you are really passionate about, it's a good thing to start. It is better to start than not to start all.

When you decide to take on a new skill or start a new training, mastering it doesn't come automatically. You do not just succeed immediately. You make mistakes until you get better at it. Let's take, for example, the story of the tortoise. It's one of the slowest animals, but it always gets to the finishing line despite all odds. That is how I look at success. Another example is human beings. After we are born, we learn to walk, talk, and pretty much all the basics during our early years until we become adults, and then we age. That is also a reflection of how I look at

---

20 "Quote by Jordan B. Peterson," Goodreads (Goodreads), accessed August 8, 2021, https://www.goodreads.com/quotes/9101272-if-you-are-not-willing-to-be-a-fool-you.

success because it does not come in one sitting. So, that is the genesis of everything. Success begins from somewhere.

Failing does not mean it's the end of the road. That is why it is said that a journey of a thousand miles begins with a step. It doesn't mean that we won't fall along the way but that we begin by trying.

Failure means being pushed. I have never stopped dreaming, even as a stay-at-home mom. I always had that urge in me to complete something. I may not have known how or where to start, but I told myself I would do it. Everyone is born with something within them that can burst at any age. It does not take something big for us to realize that we are successful; rather, it's how we feel on the inside. That moment is *your* moment. No one can take it from you. Picture a child when they start trying to walk: they fall, get up, and try again. And when they finally walk without falling, it becomes a win for them. And that is how we feel when we reach that goal point. It never ends because we want to keep going once we hit that "jackpot." That is the feeling that a child who is struggling to walk has. When they make it, you see them jump around, and each time they do something new, they want you to see how far they've come. That is a baby celebrating their big win.

Success does not mean that there will not be fear. Fear still has its place, but you have to push it away and watch where you are heading. Fear is a blessing or curse because it either pushes us to do right, or it pushes us to do wrong. You have to tell yourself that it cannot come and overshadow your plans. I still vividly remember the first time I was asked by one of my mentors to do a Facebook livestream in order to promote myself and my business. Fear immediately took hold of me. I began to ask myself a lot of questions which eventually did not help me. Video marketing has become the new norm, and it still took me time. That was me letting fear be a part of my success.

Beyond Success tells us the stories that we are unable to share with the people around us. These are the secrets you know you have within you. I know that as moms, we have a lot of success beyond what people see. A lot of times, the sacrifices moms put in are hardly recognized.

To achieve success, one has to stop overthinking and focus on the meaning of their purpose. We sometimes take situations or interpret opportunities in such a deep manner that we end up holding our own dreams. A lot of talent is held within because of our thoughts and fears. We say we are "not good enough" but fail to understand that the people we see as perfect started from somewhere and became the people we stand to beat ourselves over. No one is born perfect. We all start from the same point. The difference comes in when we can do the things other people are unwilling to do. Then, we become that mirror of the other person who we want to be.

"You cannot find yourself if you don't lose yourself."[21]

—Sri Akarshana

Sri Akarshana goes further to explain that we would never play a game without a challenge. You would never do a puzzle that was already done. The meaning behind the loss is the journey to the found. Learn to embrace the moments of failure. Stay curious about what you want to achieve with your wandering minds, and have a wonderful time while asking the right questions, as with questions comes answers.

I believe that one way to achieve success is by eliminating some of the things that we grew up hearing like, "Money doesn't grow on trees," "For success to come, one has to dig deep down and look where they want to go," "Success is not achieved in one sitting," and "Most successful people gave up time, money, and sacrificed to achieve what they have." Our traditional beliefs about success and money hold us back and limit us from achieving our dreams. Mindset is everything. From the moment you set that journey to achieve, you have to have an open mind that will lead you to where you want to go. A limited mindset will keep you from achieving, but a mindset of abundance will lead you to unexpected places.

---

21 "Download Instagram Stories of Master Sri Akarshana (@master_sri_akarshana)," StoriesDown, accessed August 8, 2021, https://storiesdown.com/users/master_sri_akarshana.

This is true because an open mind will make you find success quicker than a closed mind. A mind set to achieve will never fail because it's aware of what it has to go through. Take, for instance, a lottery winner. Most of them fail because the knowledge to set success was absent. The money disappears, and they go back broke and wonder why they failed. Thus, a cycle is handed from one generation to the next.

When success is built from within, we realize that it is achieved faster. Regardless of failure, we go back and try to achieve even better things. That is why big names like Grant Cordone say that if they failed today or lost everything, they would start again without a problem. That is because they have set a mindset that will take them anywhere, regardless of the outcome. We see this in his recent TV show *Undercover Billionaire*. It goes to show the strength of achieving success from the inside. Therefore, success is attained by digging deep—starting from the mind, the sacrifices you make, and the strength to reach the desired level.

Sometimes our success is held back because of the people we surround ourselves with or what society thinks about what they are doing. One of them is the stay-at-home mom who is looked upon as the "privileged one," or "that lazy woman," who just wants to sit around and spend money and doesn't want to work. This makes them shy away from expressing themselves or pursuing their gifts because their minds keep beating the drum that they are good at doing nothing. This brings me to the point of how everyone defines success. The stay-at-home mom defines her success by making sure that she gives her ultimate best to her children by being there for them at all times. Many of them ask the question: Why not give the best of you? This leads them on. They give to those who matter most to them.

Regardless of what we think about how success is achieved, we should bear in mind that the first rule of success is to have a vision. Without this, you will scratch the earth and not get to your destination. Vision gives you the reason to make the sacrifices you are ready to make. It wakes you up in the morning or in the middle of the night to remind you of the journey that you are taking or about to make. People who lead with a vision easily achieve success because it builds their mindset.

Vision is like a map that will lead you to your final destination, giving you clues to every exit you are about to make or decisions you want to take for yourself or your business. That is why we have heard most strong leaders talk about vision boards. I like to call them "directors" because when you have them before you, you know exactly where you're heading, what you want, and how you want it to be. It shortens the journey.

Everyone is a master of their own trade. So, success is not defined by anyone but *you*. Everyone has their own personal definition of success forged by their daily life experiences. I spent most of my early years with my grandmother. Through her, I gathered much wisdom that has helped to push me as a woman. Grandmother was a strong force. She had a strong mind to achieve whatever she wanted and was never bothered about how it was going to be done but always pushed to the end. I have carried that spirit in me, and it has helped me most of my adult life. We have seen big celebrities like Tiger Woods define success in many ways. He has failed and gotten up many times. When we set goals, we achieve them. One of the best ways of doing this is by setting a timeline. This will enable you to achieve goals faster because you do not want that time to pass you by. It pushes you to ask questions like, "How can I save lives?" and "How can I help others be where they want to be?" These questions push you because you want to be the reason why someone is smiling. Because you have set your vision. You have a goal (or mission), and then you achieve it. It becomes SUCCESS.

To be fair, failure hurts, and I believe that when you are thrown down, it means that you have to wake up strong. A lot of times, we look at people who are successful and forget that they too have failed in order to make it there. Yes, they do, and more times than we think. We clap for the glamor and cheer their elegant customs but don't know where their shoe bites them. We have read in autobiographies and stories they've shared that success does not come easy. Elon Musk might be a billionaire today, but he has failed a billion times to become a billionaire. Just like Oprah,

Jeff Bezos, Warren Baffert, Bill Gates, and many others, we can think of in our lives. "Rome wasn't built in a day." When you fail, take it as a learning experience and do not cry about it too much. The time you take to cry is the time you could have used to put things together.

Success has power, and it's a liberation. It comes with sweat and blood, but the feeling of achieving surpasses the trying moments. Let me dive deep and say it's like the moment a woman gives birth: she forgets the labor pains and rejoices about her child, and the pain is forgotten.

Anthony Robbins says, "Your destiny is determined by the choices you make. Choose now, choose well."[22] So, everything about success is 'ME.' It's YOU. It's what you want your legacy to be. It's what you want people to know you for. The beauty of success comes like a morning glory that has just bloomed. The feeling is endless. Remember, success is not an accident. With belief, courage, and willpower, you can do it. It doesn't skip steps, thereby giving you moments of building up and taking the right steps.

BIOGRAPHY

Isabella Kibunri is a busy and passionate stay-at-home mom. She is a very positive person who loves to learn and share knowledge with other people. She loves taking care of her children, traveling, problem-solving, and reading. Isabella's experience as a stay-at-home mom made her self-development skills grow as it helped to bring out her imagination. Through this, she has been able to learn skills that will help to bring out the gift of the stay-at-home mom. She has been married for sixteen years and is a mom to four beautiful children.

Connect with Isabella Kibunri via https://linktr.ee/Nyuydze

---

22 "Tony Robbins Quotes," Motivation Ping, accessed August 9, 2021, https://motivationping.com/tony-robbins-quotes/.

CHAPTER 19

Lead, Follow, Or Get Out Of The Way

By Dr. Joel Vance

It was the summer of 1980. Jimmy Carter was the President of the United States. The weather was miserable as I suffered through ninety-degree temperatures along the Potomac River in Quantico, Virginia. Most of my friends were at the lake or the beach, but I was going through ten weeks of Marine Corps Officer Candidate School. It was some of the most brutal training imaginable. Three-mile runs along with running the obstacle course was practically an everyday occurrence. My weight dropped from 210 pounds to 175 pounds in less than ten weeks.

The Summer of 1980 was the first time I had heard the phrase "Lead, follow, or get out of the way." The Marine Corps engrained this phrase into our heads and taught us that leaders set the example and lead from the front, not the rear. This phrase hit home with me, and I have tried to follow its principles for the last forty years. Most people give Thomas Payne credit for coming up with the phrase in the late 1700s. General George Patton lived by it, and most recently, Ted Turner wrote a book with the phrase as its title.

'Lead, follow, or get out of the way' means different things to different people. Good leadership is how an organization reaches its full potential. Good leaders do not try to do everything themselves but motivate and empower others to do their job. Many people incorrectly think that a leader has all the answers. Good leaders hire people who fit into their vision and strategy for their expertise and who may know more than them. Good leaders learn from their followers. Poor leaders can be a bottleneck to the organization and hinder its growth. Lee Iacocca illustrated this when he stated: "I hire people who are brighter than me and then I get out of their way."[23]

Unsurprisingly, great leaders are great followers. No matter how high our title in an organization, we report to someone. If you can neither lead nor follow, then have the common sense to get out of the way. If you know how to fix a problem or have a creative idea, then lead! If you see someone who has a great idea and could use some support, then follow! If you are impeding positive change or enforcing rules that do not make sense, then get out of the way. During my career, I have experienced good and bad leaders. I have had leaders who lead. But I have had my share of those who thought they were leading when they should have followed or got out of the way.

After the military, my first professional job was as a production supervisor at a company that made explosives for the Army. I discovered very quickly that leading as a civilian was much different from leading in the military. The company had a union which made leading even more difficult. My shift had approximately ten union employees, and our job was to pour nitroglycerin into nitrated cotton and mix it. We had to follow safety procedures precisely. My leadership philosophy had always been to treat people like you would like to be treated, but I soon discovered that this philosophy did not always yield results.

The chief operator on my shift was the union representative and a strong union supporter. I tried my normal leadership principles, and the chief operator failed to follow my direction and often rebuked me. Our production numbers were low compared to other shifts. Since he had more experience with explosives than me, I allowed him to take the lead, and I would follow him. But the results were the same. Finally, I got out of the way to see if his pride would get him back on board. Again, the results were the same. At that point, I was determined that it was my time to lead

---

23 "Lee Iacocca Quotes," BrainyQuote (Xplore), accessed June 8, 2021, https://
    www.brainyquote.com/quotes/lee_iacocca_383216.

again. I became very critical and demanding of him. I talked to him very harshly. Immediately, things turned around, and our shift became number one in production and remained there. The chief operator and I had a mutual understanding from that point on. I learned a valuable lesson that people are not motivated the same way to do their jobs.

Several years later, I took a job as a quality manager at a manufacturing company that made fused silica. At different times with the company, I reported to two different managers. One was the worst supervisor I ever had, and the other was the best supervisor I had in my career. I started out working for the director of quality, who I consider one of the worst supervisors I have worked for. It is my belief that he meant well, as he was a hard worker and wanted the company to succeed. However, he had many faults. He micromanaged every employee who worked for him and empowered no one. Any ideas I brought to him were immediately shot down. An idea I brought to him that he shot down was suggested to him by the company's CEO several weeks later. All of a sudden, my previous idea was a great one.

The CEO lived in another state and would fly in on Monday afternoons and fly out on Friday mornings. When my boss would hear the CEO arrive, we would immediately hear him running upstairs to discuss things. It was almost comical, but also pathetic. None of the other directors or managers had much of a chance to discuss issues with the CEO because my boss hogged all of his time. You would also hear him saying, '*I* did this, or '*I* did that,' unless something went wrong. Then it became '*He* did it.' I truly think he would have done anything to get to the top. He was like a driver who hogs the fast lane besides a car in the slow lane. You just want him to "get out of the way."

After working with the company for a couple of years, I was promoted to Director of Quality and Human Resources and reported to the plant manager, who was the best boss I ever had. His name is Paul Strunk, and other than being a University of Kentucky fan, he was an excellent leader. Paul listened to us, empowered us, and allowed us to live up to our potential. His direction totally turned the company around. I never saw him get angry, and he related to all of us. Paul implemented many of my suggestions that my previous boss had turned down.

One of our greatest achievements at the company was with safety. Before Paul, the company could not go a week without an OSHA reportable injury. Worker's compensation insurance was over $400,000 a year. Paul knew of my safety training at the explosives company I had previously worked for. He empowered me to put together a safety program that would drastically reduce accidents. Procedures and job safety analyses were written down. Safety audits were conducted. Training was implemented. Gradually, the OSHA reportable injuries started to decrease. We implemented safety incentives that got all the employees thinking about safety. During a brainstorming session, Paul and I came up with an idea to give away a brand-new truck to an employee if the company went a year without an OSHA reportable injury. Employees laughed when they first heard this because they thought it was an impossible goal. The first year we implemented it, the company went eleven months and one week before we had an OSHA reportable injury. We implemented it again and reached the goal the second year, and we gave away the truck. You may be asking how we afforded to implement those strategies. It paid for itself. Worker's compensation insurance had dropped from over $400,000 to under $200,000 during that time.

One of Paul's best traits was that he wanted all his employees to reach their full potential. He encouraged me to get my doctorate, for which I am very grateful. He encouraged one of his shift leaders to get his degree. This particular person was anti-college and saw no use in it. However, with Paul's encouragement, the man earned his degree, which totally changed his perspective. Currently, this man is the company's plant manager, and he would have never achieved the position without Paul's encouragement. Paul knew when to lead, when to follow, and when to get out of the way. He was a perfect example of this phrase.

A job opportunity for an Italian international company opened up several years later. I needed the experience from an international company, so I was hired as Director of Human Resources and oversaw HR in a US plant and one in Montreal, Canada. It was a diverse company with a lot of poor leadership. One of the things I despise more than anything is a person in a leadership position who will not make decisions. One in particular, at this plant, was the logistics manager. He would not make a decision if his life depended on it. His answer to anyone who asked him to make a decision was that he would have to call his boss in Canada. I am not talking about non-routine decisions, but basic routine decisions. He was definitely a follower, and we could have saved a lot of money by replacing him with a technician.

The company had supervisors who would not make decisions because they hoped problems would go away. Problems do not disappear; they only get worse. These supervisors needed to get out of the way, and soon enough, they did. Because of their lack of supervision, the positions were eliminated. I would rather have a person who made poor decisions than one who would not make one. Most people learn from their poor decisions, but you cannot learn from not making decisions.

The company Vice-President was my boss at this plant. He tried to micromanage us in every detail. One silly example was when he had his management staff in a meeting. He explained that he wanted us to carry a small spiral notebook in our pockets, pull it out, and write down if we saw something wrong when we were walking through the plant. He actually illustrated pulling the notebook out of his pocket and writing on it. I was so frustrated by his micromanagement that I spoke up and asked him if he would show us again because I did not completely understand it. Everyone laughed aloud, and I was on his bad list for months. It got so bad that many managers threatened to quit, and his boss had to reel him in.

Unlike Paul Strunk, this vice-president did not encourage us to reach our full potential. He actually told me that I did not have time to finish my doctorate and should quit. Luckily, I did not listen to him. I believe that he felt threatened by me having more of education than him. His degrees were from an elite university, and he would sometimes belittle people with degrees from less elite universities. He was not a leader or a follower. He should have just got out of the way.

Throughout my career, my leadership skills have tremendously improved. However, my career has also had its peaks and valleys. I have been a leader and follower, and there were times when I should have gotten out of the way. I have worked for good leaders and poor ones. In my opinion, the key to good leadership is to empower and trust your employees. Encourage them to reach their full potential, and by all means, do not micromanage them. Hire employees who have more expertise than you, and allow them to do their jobs. There are times when you may have to follow them, but that is not a bad thing. Like the slow driver in the fast lane, you have to know when to get out of the way.

BIOGRAPHY

Dr. Joel Vance is an Associate Professor of Business at King University. His career started with the Marine Corps, and later, he became a Naval Officer. In addition, he has held executive management positions at several different companies. He has owned several businesses and currently owns a Tutor Doctor Franchise that ranks in the top twenty-five. Dr. Vance has published several articles such as "Employee Turnover, a Management Perspective" in various business journals. His doctoral degree in business and his vast management experience helps him teach business issues that plague organizations in a way that students can relate to. He combines theory with practical applications in real-world settings. His passion for teaching allows him to mentor many students who want to be entrepreneurs or managers.

Connect with Dr. Joel Vance via https://linktr.ee/tutordoctorknoxville

CHAPTER 20

Determination And Perseverance

By Joseph Arguello

After serving as a drill sergeant in the United States Army for the last three years, I went on to sell insurance overnight. Talk about a rude awakening.

As I met with clients day after day, I began to notice that most of them didn't want to talk about insurance—only about themselves, their kids, or their grandkids.

I never talked about insurance unless they brought it up. Soon, I became the top producing agent. My district manager wanted to know how I sold so much insurance. I simply told him, "I'm not selling insurance. People are buying policies for themselves, their kids, and their grandkids." This is how I became the top producing agent. I simply learned to listen to others talk about their favorite subjects. I learned a valuable lesson during my short insurance career that would serve me for the rest of my life!

During this time, I met Elisha, and we got married and moved to Santa Fe, New Mexico. We are the proud parents of our two boys, Kyle and Sean, who have both turned into great young men!

As time went on, finances got tighter and tighter. Even though we were able to put our boys through private school, we found ourselves living paycheck to paycheck, and we no longer had extra spending money. We made a huge sacrifice to put our boys through private school. I was tired of working long hours. Elisha and I only saw each other in the morning before we left for work and a couple of hours before bedtime. I knew there had to be something better than just working for a living and paying bills. What else can we do?

I started looking for a better way to create an additional income. I transitioned from insurance sales to financial services and supplemental retirement plans. Now I had more time, and I increased our income. This is where I learned and experienced the power of residual income. Residual income pays you repeatedly. What a concept! I never knew about this. How was it that I never heard of it?

During that holiday season, I learned about "leveraged" residual income. Remember, I had residual income that was totally dependent on my efforts. I was doing everything myself. I had to service all my accounts, and the bigger my accounts grew, the more time I had to spend servicing them. Thankfully, someone introduced me to a unique way of creating a residual income by serving and helping others.

Luckily, I had a wise mentor who took me under his wings and advised me to stop doing everything myself and simply learn a few other skills. He showed me how to build a team of people and use a success system. He helped me start my journey of reading the right books and listening to audio recordings of other successful people. Most importantly, he took me to the weekly meetings and monthly training events, and we traveled to the quarterly and annual events. I realized I had a lot to learn in a short period of time. My mentor told me to work on myself and my skills.

During my journey, I began to study, practice, and teach those same skills. I sharpened my skill of listening to people. I learned how to talk to people the right way. I learned about posture and patients. I became genuinely interested in other people, but most importantly, I learned how to become the right leader. I learned to be a servant to others and use leverage to create the power of duplication, which in turn creates residual income.

I've always had big dreams and goals; I just never had the right vehicle to help me accomplish those dreams and goals!

I'm always the first one to show up and the last one to leave. The more I learn, the hungrier I get. I always introduced myself to everyone, especially the top producers and the most successful people in the room. It's true that if you're the smartest or most successful person in the room, you're in the wrong room. I do whatever I can to help serve other leaders. If they had bags, I would offer to carry their bags. I open doors for them. I would get them a good seat. I would get them something to drink. I simply made sure they were comfortable and taken care of. I became a servant leader to others. I realized that leadership isn't about me. Leadership isn't a rank, a title, or a position; leadership is who you are! Leadership is about serving and helping other people.

If I can learn a few skills, so can you! If I can learn how to create leveraged residual income, so can you! If I can learn how to help and serve other people, so can you! If I can learn to become the right leader, so can you! Your background doesn't matter. Anyone who has a burning desire can learn and master a few skills and take action to get results!

Now let me tell you about some of the struggles I personally had to go through. This doesn't mean you'll have the same struggles.

After two years of building ten percent of my company's volume, they realigned my organization, lowered team commissions, stopped paying leadership bonuses, and capped our income potential. They simply took away a huge percent of everything we built. We had to pick ourselves up, dust ourselves off, and start all over.

Many of the top leaders invited me to help them launch a new company. This was the first time I had a chance to be one of the first in a company. We launched the company and created momentum during our first fourteen months. Then the company's owner completely changed the pay plan from uni-level to binary and stopped paying leadership bonuses. We lost most of our organization, and in ninety days, it was over. Did we think of giving up or quitting? NO! We just simply picked ourselves up, dusted ourselves off, and started all over again.

Following this, several of the top leaders invited me to help them launch another new company. I had another chance to be one of the first.

Within three years of creating momentum, legal battles and negative publicity followed. Soon after, the company started replacing the corporate team and top leaders who helped build the company. After several years of building teams of customers and distributors, I found myself left without a company. We were advised to implement the six-month non-compete clause, so we waited for six long months. Did we think of giving up or quitting? NO! We waited for six months, then we picked ourselves up, and dusted ourselves off. We pushed through all the headaches and heartaches and started all over again.

After our six long months, one of the owners invited me to be one of twenty-five founding members. This time, we were backed by a multi-billionaire who owned several well-known companies. After our fly-in and private meeting at this multi-billionaire's home, we knew we had something special—something unique in the industry.

As my partners and I continued to build the company, our teams and our accounts grew, and we started to create momentum. Well, guess what? Not again! On our one-year anniversary, without warning, the company closed. I mean, they just stopped. They just shut down everything! No products. No commissions. No explanation. No answers. Just like that, it was over!

I was at a point in my life where I had a hard time trusting any owner, CEO, or corporate executives! I was losing more and more friendships and partnerships because, once again, owners or corporate executives were making wrong decisions. I questioned myself: "Why does this keep happening? Why is this part of my journey? Why do I go through all these ups and downs? Why? There must be a reason for all of this. Do I need to quit and walk away or keep looking? Do I keep searching? What do you do? I mean, what would you do?"

Low and behold, within two weeks, one of the top leaders from the company that just closed invited me to help him launch a new company. 'Here we go again!' I thought. As you can tell, I was fed up with all the lies and promises by that time. I told him that I wasn't just interested in starting all over again with the hopes of making it work in a new company.

I was *frustrated*! I mean, *frustrated* was an understatement! I was beyond mad! I was upset!

I told him I'd only be interested in starting over and launching another company if he was starting his own company! He told me he was, and it had to do with philanthropy. You know, the concept of giving and receiving. I understand philanthropy; I've been doing that for the last several years with several companies. Now, remember, our company had closed two weeks before, so I was, at least, open to look because we were all just left out in the cold! What was I going to do? Quit? Give up? Throw in the towel? NO!

Remember, I needed to find a home. A place where I could build a team of customers and distributors. A place where I could continue to help others create a leveraged residual income. So, for that reason, I needed all the details. I wanted to know everything, so we had several phone calls with him and the other owner. After that, I decided to partner up and help them launch and build a new global team.

Wow! To our surprise, everything was working. It was growing. People were really excited, and we were finally making a difference! After six short months of long hours, phone calls, three-way calls, conference calls, and webinars, we started creating momentum. This was a dream come true! Around the eighth month, one of the owners—yes, one of the owners—decided to change the company that we helped launch and build. Within thirty days, he turned it into something else. I found myself in the same situation once again. All those people were left out in the cold! Do I give up? Do I quit? What should I do? What would you do?

After all my new company launches and starting over, I decided to find an existing and successful company.

I decided to ask for:

- the right solutions
- the right company
- the right leadership
- the right corporate team

By asking for the right things, I put the "Law of Attraction" to work.

The right leadership with the right solutions found me!
The right company with the right corporate team found me!
The right company with the right pay plan structure found me!

Once again, I was proud and excited to have the opportunity to help others create a "leveraged" residual income with a company that had a successful track record. I no longer had to question the integrity of the owners or the corporate team members. I no longer had to worry if we're going to make it or possibly close down!

I learned some of the most important lessons on this journey:

Don't Stop! Don't Quit! Don't Give Up! Keep Looking!
Keep Searching! Keep Asking, and You Shall Receive!

If you're currently in a company, bless others with it.
If you're looking for an established company, keep looking.
If someone invites you to look, please take a look; it might just change your life forever!

Thank you for allowing me to share my unique and frustrating story! I would also like to thank all the people who participated with us along the way. My journey is far from over; failure is just part of it!

It's true—if I can do it, so can you!

"Leadership isn't a pin, rank, or title. Leadership is who you are"
—Joseph Arguello

BIOGRAPHY

Joseph Arguello is known for his dedication, persistence, and unique teaching and training techniques. He has helped launch several direct selling companies and assisted others in building large teams. Joseph became a certified trainer and has taught and trained thousands of other independent business owners throughout his career. Because of Joseph's U.S. Army Drill Sergeant background, he is one of the best presenters and trainers in his profession. He keeps everything on an elementary level so everyone can learn, understand, take action, and get results. His unique teaching style makes things simple and easy to understand. Joseph has been married to Elisha since 1993. They are blessed with two sons, Kyle and Sean.

Connect with Joseph Arguello via https://lifechangingoptions.info/

CHAPTER 21

A Life's Journey To Become An Overnight Success

By Leonie Hunt

I have always known that my ultimate success would come in my latter years. That is when I would have the most significant impact.

For most of my working life, I did not look for security. I was happy to spend what I earned, travel, be the party girl, charitably give and support others, and do many other things that I probably should not have done. However, I had a lot of fun doing it!

I believe that the impossible becomes possible if declared and accepted as a fait accompli. There have been many instances where this has occurred to me. I call them my "Barbra Streisand" moments, as seeing Barbra in concert was one of my "impossible dreams" that I just knew would happen. In March 2000, it did.

I have always believed that I have been put on this earth for a reason, but I must admit that as I have made my way through life, with its many ups and downs, I often found it difficult to fathom just exactly what that reason was.

In retrospect, as a true entrepreneur, I found success elusive and always felt inferior comparing myself to others. As a result, I hid behind the words "I'm fine" as I experienced one challenge after another because I was embarrassed that I never quite *made it.*

My "Light Bulb" moment took place only recently, when after living a life-craving success, I finally realised that I am the epitome of success.

__I am courageous__, often stepping into the unknown with faith and conviction, just knowing everything will work out.

__I am resilient__, repeatedly proving that I can bounce back from many failures, setbacks, disappointments, challenges, and even betrayals I have experienced over my nearly sixty years.

__I am persistent__ in my quest to find what is right for me and to keep trying until I find it.

__*True success is the will to keep trying as your authentic self, with grace and integrity. That is how I have lived and continue to live my life.*__

A very dear friend once told me that everything in life is either a gift or a lesson. Of course, that made perfect sense to me, until I realised that I was particularly good at learning the lessons but not so good at receiving the gifts.

When I finally started receiving the gifts and allowing people to give to me, my life changed for the better.

But let us start at the beginning, so you know what makes me tick!

My formative early years were full of happiness. I was the apple of my parents' eyes. I loved to sing and dance, and I was everyone's friend and favourite girl. Apparently, at the age of three, I even stood up and sang "We All Live in a Yellow Submarine" at a Beatles movie at the top of my voice, much to everyone's delight. I was always keen to put on performances and shows for the family.

When I was five years old, my life dramatically changed! My much anticipated, and longed-for little sister was tragically born with cerebral palsy. At the time, I had no idea how her birth was going to impact my life. It did not take long for the young five-year-old me to feel that I did not deserve to be happy when my little sister was faced with a terrible life of struggle and sickness and would never reach her full potential. In a heartbeat, even at five years old, I just knew that I had to look after myself and learn to be strong and independent.

I loved and adored my little sister, but with all the focus on her care and needs, my little life at the time descended into one of isolation and loneliness. The decision to become strong and independent had a massive impact on my whole life. I tried to make up for the unfairness of life by overcompensating and putting others first rather than myself. This was where my life of service began.

I loved the limelight and was a bit of a show pony, always putting on a brave, happy face, and going out of my way to make others feel better. But deep inside, I kept the real me protected, hidden, thinking that if I did, no one could hurt me.

I lived in Jamestown, a small country town in the mid-north of South Australia, in a working-class family, with my parents believing my life would be best served as a wife and a mother and that "a woman's place was in the home." While that was a common theme with little girls growing up in the sixties and seventies, I did not see that as my future at the time and decided that I had other plans. I started working at the local news agency for two years before commencing with a career in nursing.

In my early twenties, I moved to Adelaide, the capital of South Australia, to study drama, which was my true love. Like many young girls, I entertained exciting thoughts that I would one day be discovered and become a world-famous actress. Imagine a naïve country girl auditioning for a place at a renowned university with a lot of passion. But sadly, I did not have an appropriate audition piece. It was not meant to be, so I continued nursing for another few years until one day, I woke up and decided that I had enough of this sickness in my life.

In the mid-eighties, I tried to resign. Fortunately, I was instantly offered administration duties instead, which led to a purchasing and supply role for the hospital where I worked. Little did I know that this was the start of my management career.

At that time, I met and eventually married a great guy who, unbeknown to me, had been hiding his alcohol addiction. Of course, he was a wonderful man, one that everybody loved—but that was when he was sober! When he was drunk, he turned into a monster! A vile, violent drunkard who would shame me, beat me, and make me feel pathetic and worthless, and worst of all, helpless. Of course, he had the uncanny ability to turn on the charm to all his friends and family, convincing them I was the problem.

The destructive nature of his words cut me to the core with phrases like "You put your career before me" and "You are a lousy wife!" When he hit me, he was always careful to make sure that the bruises were in places that were not obvious and could be covered up easily. Many times, I remember putting on a brave face and being ultra-careful not to let my family, friends, or work colleagues know what was going on. I was protecting them from my reality, as I knew they would not cope or understand why I put up with this. I thought I was trying to help him, to cure him of his dreadful addiction. After all, I married him for better or worse, in sickness and in health. When I eventually faced reality, I realised that in this marriage, he was "sick," and this was for "worse!"

I felt such a burden of responsibility and that this was my mess to fix, and nobody could help me do that. To make matters even worse, I was so embarrassed, humiliated, fragile, and overwhelmed by my desperately unhappy situation that I lost sight of reality during this time.

I finally found the courage to leave my husband—not because of what he had been doing to me, but what I nearly did to him! I woke up one night with a knife in my hand, about to slash his throat! In that instant, I knew I had experienced insanity! He had pushed me to the edge of my endurance, and in a moment of clarity, I knew I needed to leave before I did something I would regret for the rest of my life.

After I left, he stalked me, turning up to my work, drunk and having to be taken away by the police. I cannot describe the intensity of the shame I felt, but it did become the catalyst for the biggest move in my life.

At the time, the hospital I worked for helped me with a job at a start-up purchasing corporation for hospitals in Sydney, the largest capital in Australia. Although truly thankful, I could not believe this opportunity of a lifetime was mine for the taking, and it meant that I could get away from all the mess associated with my ex-husband and start a new life.

I knew this was going to be a massive challenge. I was so scared about having to drive to Sydney, which was some 1,300 km away from Adelaide, on my own, yet everyone just assumed I had taken it in my stride. And, of course, I put on my brave face. Thank goodness for a colleague who offered to drive over with me and fly back. He was the only one who seemed to know how I was feeling. I knew no one in Sydney and was going to live with a friend of a friend. I guess, in hindsight, the actress in me portrayed that I had it all under control.

This was, to date, my biggest challenge. Yet, I did it. I felt the fear and did it anyway! In some respects, it was the most exciting time of my life. But again, it was also the loneliest. Although I was used to isolation, living in Sydney was where I experienced gut-wrenching loneliness, particularly at night. Thank goodness an Adelaide wholesale distribution company with whom I was negotiating asked me whether I was interested in returning to Adelaide. I jumped at the chance, and so began my next chapter in the corporate world.

My working life has been a journey where I have worked in all types of businesses over the years, ranging from corporate to small business, from nursing and sales to management, and to national management and general management positions.

I did not like corporate life! I did not like backstabbing or politics of any type. Back in the 1990s, women were still being treated as lesser beings. I was expected to be both the manager and my secretary. Yet, I still managed to achieve outstanding growth for my division while maintaining my truth, integrity, openness, and honesty. These traits did not sit well in the corporate arena or with playing the political game just to survive. I was betrayed and let down by people I employed and nurtured—those who wanted to climb the corporate ladder. They took advantage of my perceived weaknesses, which I now know are strengths.

This was the catalyst to starting my own business, where I could say yes or no on my terms!

However, it did mean giving up a lot, particularly the security of a handsome salary and benefits package, so I could find myself and operate on my terms to help others.

Great plans, but then reality struck. You do need money to live! So, for the next twenty years, I became an employee, again, in various roles: General Management, Business Development, Sales and Marketing, and then part-time as a Marketing Consultant. During this time I still operated my digital marketing business part-time and then returned full time in 2020.

The last ten years have been particularly challenging, with many ups and downs, including an ongoing battle with depression, losing my dad, two bouts of breast cancer resulting in bilateral mastectomies, and the body ravaging treatments that followed. While going through chemotherapy, my partner's son was also fighting a losing battle with cancer, so there was limited support from him at the time (when I needed him most). Eventually, his son lost the battle, and my relationship did not survive such a juggernaut of tragedy that came at both of us. I was trying to manage the grief of my own situation, while trying to help him with his grief (and mine) for his son. I organised professional help for him, which was not appreciated, so he left me during one of the most difficult times of my life! That was a big blow, and that was a tough one from which to rebuild and move forward with my life.

In early 2021, things changed for the better when I became a Born-Again Christian. Finally, I did not feel lonely anymore, and I knew that I would never be again. My faith now gives me courage and conviction to stand proudly as the person I am and that my life's journey is as it should be. I have finally found the reason why I have been put on this earth. God has always had a plan for me, and I just needed to let the Holy Spirit in. What an astounding difference this has made in my life. I now see myself as others have all my life: a model of service and leadership and an inspiration to help others become their true selves and embrace their life journey. The big difference, now, is that I am not alone anymore.

Many more chapters have occurred and still remain in my life, and I am excited for the future and what it holds.

I hope that in sharing my story of never giving up, you may find the strength and resilience to live your own life's journey and fulfil your true potential as the courageous and authentic person you are. Remember, nothing can stop you! When you do things for the right reasons and with integrity and authenticity, you have the power to lead, influence, and help more people than you could ever think possible.

BIOGRAPHY

Leonie Hunt is known for two things: generosity and perseverance. Her initiative and results have been the foundation of her business success. A practical and common-sense approach, together with an outstanding ability to build relationships with people, has given her the unique opportunity to operate at strategic and operational levels within several small businesses and large corporations. These roles include general management, sales and marketing, customer service, leadership development, purchasing, and logistics. She has earned her stripes in the "School of Life," survived domestic violence, two bouts of breast cancer, the deaths of dearly loved family members, and a breakup with the love of her life. It is fair to say she has lived a life full of setbacks, disappointments, betrayals, sadness, and loss. However, she has learned that success is all about getting up and moving forward despite whatever you may be facing.

Connect with Leonie Hunt via https://linktr.ee/leoniehunt

CHAPTER 22

Don't Give Up On God Because He Hasn't Given Up On You!

By Margaret Camacho

Have you ever felt like you were dropped into the deep end of the pool without a life jacket or flotation device? I guess I have felt that way most of my life but pressed on regardless.

I guess most people would say I grew up as a tomboy. My first memory goes back to when I was about six; I was always involved, being the only girl around all the boys. There were ten of us, and nine were boys; of course, I was the only girl. Did this make me want to be better than the boys? You bet it did! Learning to ride a bicycle is one of the memories that stands out. My dad was the manager of a bank in British Guiana, where four of five of us were born. So, it was great to have him teach me to ride on the road outside our house above his branch. Little did I know that he would let go of the bike when he felt I could pedal on my own. So, when I looked back to ask how I was doing, I was shocked to see that I was pedaling away on my own, and he was standing way back with a big smile on his face, saying, "You're doing great, just keep pedaling!" Well, utter panic took hold of me, and the next thing I knew, I was heading straight into the canal on the side of the road. So much for my riding lesson! Thankfully my dad and Akbar, the bank's night watchman, who had just arrived, fished me and my bike out of the canal; I was covered in moss and water lilies. My mum and older brother, who didn't know how to ride a two-wheeler, were looking out from the front window of the house with my baby sister. I had to be hosed off and taken up the backstairs, through the kitchen, and to the shower so I could clean up. The following week, we were awakened by Akbar, the night watchman, shouting, "We got it! We got it!" only to find that a six-foot-long alligator had crawled out of the canal and was in the drain under our bedroom windows. Whew, was I glad I did not meet him when I took the plunge with my bike?

The next memory is of my mum dressing me in a dress, of all things, to go to Mass on Sunday, and most of the parishioners, saying, "Look, the boy is a girl!" I guess I gave them a shock as they always thought I was one of the boys. That never stopped me from switching back to shorts and a t-shirt after Mass. I would always jump the fence to go next door while my older brother, the gentleman, walked around and came through the front gate. By the time my brother arrived, I was already playing with the two boys next door.

After so many experiences and my faith formation in British Guiana, my dad was transferred to St. Lucia to open the country's first branch for the bank he worked at. There began some of the happiest moments of my childhood and our family life, as we all fondly remember. That was where my youngest sister and the last of my siblings joined the family. From St. Lucia, my older brother and I were taken to boarding schools in England—my brother to my dad's alma mater, and I continued my faith formation and education at my mum's alma mater. Once again, I was dumped into the deep end with no life jacket! My faith expanded, and I am thankful to God for being in my life as I know He did not give up on me, although, at times, I am sure I was about to give up on Him, being young and having to make decisions on my own.

One of my proudest moments was when I was elected house captain for one of the three houses at school, and our greatest accomplishment was winning the sports cup, which our house had not won for many years. We did it together as a team! During my schooling in England, I spent an Easter vacation in France and lived with a French family in the Burgundy region: another eye-opening experience. I attended a week of

French school (lycée), as they went back to school before I did. It was great learning the different routines and classes, and of course, the food. I loved the "pain au chocolat," which was served as a snack.

Leaving England after six years of school and returning back to my family, who were in Trinidad then, I began life and work, as university was not an option for a woman in those days. My older brother returned to London and became a successful architect. He currently lives in Trinidad with his two sons. I have to say that God never gave up through all my experiences, and I learned to rely on Him during my darkest moments—ten years and a couple in Barbados, during the tumultuous period of Black Power in Trinidad. Shortly after our return to Trinidad, my parents moved the family to the U.S. Unfortunately, my older brother and his family could not migrate with us, as the U.S had changed its immigration laws. If you were over the age of twenty-one and unmarried, you could be sponsored. Lucky for my sister and me, but not our older brother and his family. Our family was living in two different countries again!

On our arrival to the U.S., Florida became our home. Beginning work in Miami, my life continued with jobs at Fortune 500 companies, and corporate was quite an education in itself. All thanks, once again, to God, who did not give up on me. Having lived through the start of the Black Power Days in Trinidad, it was sad to see Miami and the U.S. going through problems with race. The color of my skin did not come into play in my life in the Caribbean until the changes in Trinidad, and neither had the differences in religion. So, besides all the other things I had to get used to, it was quite a test for me. Thank God I had my faith, on which I relied heavily. God is Good, and He carried me through many moments of trial.

Becoming a parent was one of my happiest memories, and although I became a single parent when my son was only six months old, I managed to go on and decided to go back to a more stable job with regular hours. Once more, I was dumped into the deep end with no life jacket. I worked in an industry where I had no experience. After gaining some experience in the industry and making some valuable contacts, I changed jobs and ventured back into Miami to a well-established company and a position that had use for my knowledge and experience. However, the commute was longer. My son and I were in the market for a home of our own. With faith and my boss's help, our wish came true, and we settled into our new home. I continued to volunteer at our church and assisted with religious education classes. Then, I moved on to teaching with an assistant for a total of nine years. I also graduated from a two-year program of lay ministry and enjoyed learning more about my faith. This prompted me to attend the class to become a Eucharistic Minister and then volunteer to take Communion to the homebound members of the parish and those in our local hospital. I always felt much better after visiting the sick and homebound.

Unfortunately, working in Miami was not without peril. An incident took place that is ingrained in my memory. When I arrived at work one morning, I was held at gunpoint, choked, and my purse, containing my ID, driver's license, credit cards, and money that I had collected for a charity, was stolen. Luckily, I had just put my keys in my jacket pocket, so they were not in my purse. The thief had made his escape by the time the police arrived, followed by one of our technicians, who luckily turned back when the guy pointed the gun at him and told him to stop. God is good and protected us from harm. Shaken up, I went into the office, and my boss insisted that I go home. I made an appointment to replace my driver's license, and after that, I went home.

Life continued until another dark experience found its way into my life. My son had fallen in with the wrong crowd in high school, and his life began to spiral out of control. The more I prayed, the more it seemed that God was not listening. I prayed until I felt that I couldn't pray anymore. Luckily the prayer group I belonged to at our church had some amazing prayer warriors, and they prayed for us when I couldn't. It felt as though I was on autopilot for many months, possibly years. I even lost weight I could not afford to lose. Thank goodness for my doctor and his staff for their care during this time, as well as all my friends, coworkers, and prayer team. I guess God doesn't give you more than you can handle! I thank

God my son found his way back after many rough years. He has graduated from college and is now working in his field and enjoying life.

During that time, I started attending Tony Robbins' live events and was blown away at how Tony was able to help the attendees make positive changes in their lives. I even "Stepped Up" and did the Firewalk Experience at my first live event and was surprised that I was able to walk across a very hot fire pit without burning the soles of my feet. Then, in July 2004, I took a real leap of faith and attended Tony's Life Mastery event on the beautiful island of Vieques, just off Puerto Rico. What a transforming experience for me!

Climbing to the top of a telephone pole with my team shouting out words of encouragement to me was a superhuman feat because I was over fifty during that time, and I really did not think I would be able to complete the task. I finally made it to the top of the pole and had to stand on the top, with the beautiful view of the ocean; I saw St. Thomas, USVI in the distance, with my teammates below, many of whom were half my age or certainly a lot younger than me. I then did another exhilarating thing, and bungee jumped off the top of the pole to the waiting welcome of my teammates and other members of the event. Thank God for the well-secured harness and the crew securing each person before their climb. Some group members did not climb, so I was super pleased with my accomplishment. Another awesome memory from that trip was visiting the bioluminescent pool at the other end of the island, which we did in the wee hours of the night, and kayaking out to the pool (another new experience for me). Wow! The colors of the water were awesome.

In early 2020, my life took an unexpected turn due to unforeseen medical challenges and over a week in the hospital with aspiration pneumonia in March 2020. At the start of April 2020, after twenty-eight years of working in Miami, I became unemployed due to the global pandemic and lockdown of our state and country.

Life goes on, and God is close by and seeing me through my challenges. Perseverance is the key, and we need to keep putting one foot in front of the other so that the everyday challenges don't get us down. With the help of great faith, friends, and medical professionals, I am fighting the medical diagnosis of an incurable auto-immune disease. God will provide. And with all-natural supplements and a drastic change in diet, I am feeling better every day, with no signs of the disease progressing.

BIOGRAPHY

Margaret Camacho is a very caring person with a deep faith in God! She believes that all people should be given the opportunity to follow their dreams and achieve whatever they set their minds to. Having attended many self-development events and read many books, she believes that perseverance and hard work are essential in achieving your goals. Two of her favorite Bible verses are, "If God is for us, who can be against us?" and "With God, all things are possible." For these reasons, Margaret believes that we should not give up on God, as he has not given up on us. Margaret lives in South Florida. She has one son who is an engineer living in Utah.

Connect with Margaret Camacho via https://linktr.ee/Margaret.A.Camacho

CHAPTER 23

When Life Shakes You To Your Core

By Maricela DeMarco

As I sit here recalling my childhood in what was considered a third-world country, and now a developing country, even amid poverty, I was a happy child for the most part until childhood trauma struck me. As a young girl, growing up without a father, I experienced sexual abuse by someone close to me—someone I trusted. I remember becoming rebellious, promiscuous, and angry.

I was twelve years old when my mother, siblings, and I migrated to California. By then, I was full of anger. Going into my teenage years, I hated people. I felt ashamed, dirty, and not worthy to be loved after the terrible experience I had. I found refuge in a small group of friends in an LA gang. You guessed it right, I began craving the gangster lifestyle and started dressing and acting the part, becoming a "Chola." I know now that it was the attention and sense of acceptance that I craved, not the "gangster lifestyle."

I sought love in all the wrong places and with the wrong people. I soon became a high school dropout and a pregnant teenager. At the time, I was so afraid and knew little about life. But I knew this one thing: I would love my baby, and I would make sure nothing terrible happened to her as it happened to me.

On April 25, 1993, I experienced the greatest gift God and life could've given me. I became a mother for the first time, giving birth to a beautiful, healthy baby girl: my Valerie. Little did I know, this baby would change my life forever. I was not ready to be a mother. I didn't even know I wanted to be a mother. But God knew what He was doing when He let me experience motherhood.

When I knew I was expecting my first child, I began working full time in a warehouse, packing items. I developed a hunger and a drive to give my child what I didn't have as a kid, raised by a struggling single mom and barely having the essentials. Seeing my mother struggle and sacrifice to make ends meet, I promised myself that I would give my children the opportunities I didn't have: the extras in life, sports, toys, vacations, and most importantly, my time. At the same time, I made a promise to one day reward my mother for every sacrifice she made for my siblings and me.

I began my entrepreneurship, taking every opportunity that was available to me. At the time, these were with Avon, Marykay, and Tupperware. I even sold clothes and perfumes from the trunk of my car. In retrospect, I know those experiences served a purpose and prepared me for something bigger.

Fast forward a few years later, my failing marriage became a difficult learning experience; it was full of struggles and, oddly enough, happiness. I found myself in Las Vegas, Nevada. I was alone with my beautiful Valerie (six years old at the time) and my sweet Crystal (five months old). Going through a nasty divorce, I spent my first Easter in this new city. I didn't know anyone here. We slept on the floor in an empty apartment and barely had any food in the fridge. I had to leave both my girls with total strangers to watch them, so I could go to work to barely make ends meet. I loved my girls more than life itself, and I was working hard to provide a better life for them. But it seemed like no matter what I did, I couldn't get ahead, and I was reliving my childhood. But this time, I was the mother, not the child.

Even though I was not religious or spiritual by any stretch of the imagination, I always believed in a higher power. And at this low point in my life, I cried out to God, asking Him to make Himself real to me and that if He did, I would spend the rest of my life giving praise to Him.

God answered, and everything began to change. I spent the following thirteen years of my life learning and spreading the word of Christ, and I became a living testimony of what God's power could do in someone's broken life.

Shortly after, I married a wonderful and supportive man, and I became a mom for the third time, having my sassy daughter, Samantha. I had a job that paid well and a beautiful home. I thought life was great. I became obsessed with learning the Scriptures and what some would consider radical: I spent so much time away from home. My family began to fall apart. I was forced to leave the US and return to my home country, Mexico. I was a stranger in my own land. For reasons out of my control, I spent almost two years there. Life shook me once again when my oldest daughter Valerie decided she wouldn't join me in Mexico. She stayed behind and lived with her father.

After my return to the US, Valerie reunited with the rest of the family. Little did I know that the Valerie who returned to me was no longer the sweet, happy, innocent girl I left behind. I noticed Valerie was hurting and hiding a deep pain that she self-medicated with alcohol. The years to come were incredibly heartbreaking and wore our souls. A life that was once brilliant, promising, and full of happiness was now deteriorating.

I became painfully obsessed and codependent on Valerie. I tried to do everything I could to support her without enabling her, but sometimes, I felt like I was an enabler.

It didn't seem like Valerie even tried to overcome alcoholism, but looking back now, I know Valerie did all she could. She struggled and fought hard every single day to stay sober. I searched for ways to learn, cope with, and understand what she was going through. I read books and attended meetings with her. Every time Valerie would relapse, our relationship deteriorated. The problem was my perspective and rooted belief that alcoholism was a choice, not a chronic illness. It wasn't until I understood and saw the illness for what it was—an illness, not a choice—that I began to understand and educate myself on the subject. We began to restore our relationship. Having this understanding allowed me to communicate and support her on a higher level with love and more compassion than ever before. Don't get me wrong, I always loved my daughter, but I was always judging her, so she hated my approach.

Thanks to my wonderful friend, I finally started to see hope. She began to coach me and taught me metaphysics. My worldviews, beliefs, and perspectives took a radical turn, and I began to grow. I invested in self-development. I became a certified mindset and life coach, and my relationship with my children and husband drastically improved.

I had gone on a girls' getaway trip to California with a group of wonderful friends. I didn't know this at the time, but those days would be my last "normal" days.

After coming back from my girls' trip, I went back to my routine. I checked on my daughter Valerie via text; she didn't respond, but it didn't seem odd since she sometimes wouldn't respond. I didn't worry because she told my mom that she wasn't feeling well and needed to sleep, which wasn't unusual behavior from her.

But after not hearing from my daughter for a few days, I decided to check on her. Then, a parent's worst nightmare came to life: my beautiful child was in her home, unresponsive. I ran to hold her lifeless body one last time while my brain was trying to process the unimaginable. My heart tried to escape out of my chest, and I was trying to memorize her every detail—her face, hair, hands, and scent—while giving her CPR till the first responders arrived. I knew deep in my heart and soul that my child was gone.

That moment has imprinted itself onto my memory. This is an image I will carry forever, not because I welcome it, but because it shows up unexpectedly, uninvited, and unannounced. Just as Valerie's birth changed my life forever, her death also changed my life forever. Her death left my life full of broken dreams and millions of questions to which I will never have the answers: the what if's; the guilt; the blame; and the anger.

After years of being a woman of faith, I questioned my faith . . . I questioned God.

You know those moments where the world seems to crack open, and you never see things the same way ever again? This was one of those moments. This was when life shook me to my core, and every single cell in my body cried in pain. The immense loss of my firstborn, my first love, my first everything has been the most heartbreaking, chest-crushing, gut-wrenching, breath-stealing, and most debilitating challenge I had to go through.

Losing a child of any age is an indescribable journey of survival and coping with their absence brings up every emotion imaginable. Grieving carries no rules, and time becomes insignificant in so many ways. This has been my personal experience.

The sorrow of losing a daughter or son will never lessen, and yet I can tell you that it will change. You will regain your life in your own time, only if you refuse to give up. You will find a way to survive and live around the emptiness and pain. It won't suffocate you as much as it does right now. If you choose to take steps to heal your inner self, you will find joy once again.

Through my experience, I've learned that a grieving parent's worst nightmare is for their child's life to be forgotten and to be able to move forward without guilt or survivor's syndrome. We want their memory to live on. We want everyone that met them to remember that they *lived* and brought so much love and joy into this world—that they were loved so deeply.

How did I navigate through the deepest sorrow of my life?

I voted to take my time. I didn't rush the process. I allowed myself to sit in the emptiness and gave grief time to *unfold*. I allowed myself to be under construction. I dedicated most of my time to *really* exploring self-love, self-care, prayer, meditation, reiki, sound vibrational healing, and yoga. I didn't allow myself to lose sight of what my two other daughters were experiencing. They had lost their older sister, and they needed me and needed my strength. I decided to get up every morning, even if I didn't want to leave my bed and put one foot in front of the other.

I have met so many parents walking this same unbearable journey, and most of them want this to be over as if there is a time limit to grieve and move on. Please hear me out. There is no limit or expiration date to grieving. Grieving is a *powerful* emotion—as powerful as *love*. There is nothing wrong with love, so there shouldn't be anything wrong with grieving and honoring the precious memory of our beloved children.

How you choose to honor your son or daughter is your choice. I choose to honor my daughter Valerie by making it my mission to empower, inspire, and bring hope to other parents and readers who might be traveling on a similar road and experiencing a similar journey by learning how to let go of any blame, by learning to smile and laugh again, by choosing to speak her name and tell stories of her life, by choosing to share my journey of healing, and by choosing to *create* and pursue my dream job.

When, and not *if*, life shakes you to your core, how will you respond to adversity? I believe everyone has or will experience some type of traumatic event in their lives. I firmly believe that life is ten percent 'what happens to you' and ninety percent 'how you respond to it.'

BIOGRAPHY

Maricela DeMarco is a co-author of *Everyday Woman's Guide To Doing What You Love*, a speaker, and a self-made businesswoman. She is a certified mindset and spiritual coach, reiki practitioner, and a small business owner of a virtual assistant services and E-com store. She is a mother of three beautiful girls and a proud wife to her supportive husband. She loves meditation, self-development, and all practices related to self-care and self-love. She shares with the world her personal experience on how she navigated through adversity and found a new normal to move forward and continue living after the most painful, soul-crushing, and heartbreaking experience of losing a child. Her mission is to bring awareness and normalize grief. When she is not working on her self-development, you can find her on her social media, supporting and inspiring others to live and become their best selves. Deepak Chopra, her favorite author on alternative healing methods, says: "Even when you think you have your life all mapped out, things happen that shape your destiny in ways you might never have imagined." She hopes you leave this chapter inspired, motivated, and full of hope, learning how to let go of the life you had mapped out and successfully navigate through what you might never have imagined.

Connect with Maricela DeMarco via https://linktr.ee/MaricelaDeMarco

CHAPTER 24

I Am a Survivor!

By Marisa Rico

With all the damage my ex had created for me, I was heartbroken that I lost custody and that he could do all this damage while I wasn't even nearby. I felt like I was never going to see my son again or even have the chance to visit. I didn't even know where I would start.

I lived in a small town called Crownpoint, New Mexico. I met a very attractive man, who was a few years older than me. He had a lot of girls chasing after him, but he chose me. I was a fifteen-year-old dropout and thought I knew everything about being a grown-up. His parents disapproved of our relationship, but he moved in with my family and me. Not long after, I was pregnant with our son. We were excited, but there were some challenges with the morning sicknesses and mood swings. I was having a hard time eating and not gaining weight with the pregnancy. The physical abuse started three months into the pregnancy. Our relationship started to crumble, and I thought everything was my fault. His drinking started to get out of hand. He would twist my wrist to hurt me. I wanted to end the relationship, but he was threatening to fight for custody over my baby. I felt trapped and didn't really know what to do. So, I stayed.

The longer I stayed, the more controlling, jealous, and abusive he became. The abuse wasn't only physical but verbal, sexual, financial, and emotional. I was going to work black and blue and lied about who I was fighting. I tried moving away from him. I enrolled in college to work on my GED. I also put in an application for Housing Assistance which got approved a month later. I had started to receive assistance. My mom watched my son during the day.

Not long after that, my boyfriend moved in with us. He was not working, and the only income we had was my assistant check and food stamps. My schooling was during the day, and I worked at night. I was dealing with my boyfriend's alcohol abuse and walking on eggshells every day. I did whatever I could to avoid any arguments with him. He did get jobs here and there but would blame me for losing them. I really did not know how to cope and was barely over the age of eighteen. Most of the time, I would support his habits. I tried going to church regularly, but that didn't seem to help.

One night we started arguing, and I did not want him punching me, so I grabbed an empty beer bottle and broke it on his head. It cut his head open. This scared both of us. He was in shock and refused to go to the hospital. He laid down on the couch and went to sleep. I was so scared that night I fell asleep in the room. The following day, I finally talked him into going to the hospital to get stitches. I felt so bad about that incident that I started drinking with him. From there, our drinking started getting out of hand; we fought just about every night.

He would ask his family for money, lying to them about bills that needed to be paid. They did not trust him with the money, so they would hand it to me. Once I got the money, he would ask me to hand it over to him.

When my son was three years old, he was with my mom in Smith Lake. My son tried to hitchhike from mom's place to his other grandma's house in Crownpoint. When his dad found out about this, my son was spanked by the handle of the broom. Because of fear of him, I failed to protect my son and allowed him to hurt him physically.

With all the fights and arguments going on. I started to get fed up with the abuse. I did not want to be a punching bag anymore. Many times, I would do my best to protect myself by standing up to him. There were times I went to jail as well. I would get charged with domestic violence or an assault on a household member. I was sometimes taken to the hospital for my injuries. I started looking for a way to get out. It seemed impossible because of all the threats and lies he was telling me. I felt trapped, and at times, suicide was my only other option.

One day a friend of ours started coming around. He was a very good friend, and I knew him before my boyfriend. I started to feel safe with him being around and did not want him to leave. I started to see my way out of the toxic relationship. We were very good friends before, and I figured I would reconnect where we left off. He knew our situation and kept telling me to leave him.

It took the loss of two family members to finally see a way out. After the funeral, he wanted to drink when I got home. I was very upset. I started an argument with him that led to him choking me so bad that I thought I was going to die that night. But the cops got in the house just in time and arrested him for domestic violence and had a warrant for his arrest. I made my decision right there that it was time to leave. I was told that he would be in jail for some time and would not be getting out any time soon.

With all of the drinking, fighting, and the cops being called, my son was placed into protective custody. When I finally left, my friend and I moved to Nevada. We were working and doing our best to move on. While I was in Nevada, I learned that my ex gained custody, claiming I was abusing him, and managed to get him and our son in a protection home. He had me charged with assault on a household member when I was not even in the same state. I had a warrant out for my arrest due to not appearing before court.

With all the damage that my ex had created for me, I was heartbroken that I lost custody, and he was able to do all this damage while I was not even nearby. I felt like I was never going to see my son again or even have the chance to visit. I didn't even know where I would start.

We returned home over Thanksgiving, and the night before we were supposed to return to Nevada, my ex showed up at my mom's house with our son. I was shocked to see that he was driving around drunk with my son. I quickly took my son out of his car and into the house, and I told him to go home, come back in the morning, and pick him up when he sobered up, but he refused and ended up crashing his car that night. My mom took my son just to keep him safe. The following day, I went to the Crownpoint PD to get custody of my son. Our plans to go back to Nevada were quickly changed to getting custody of my son. I was given temporary custody of him. This was my opportunity, and I was going to fight for my son.

I got myself a lawyer. He advised us that we needed to quit drinking, get a job, a place to live, and a reliable car. I also needed to go to counseling and work on getting my driver's license back! I was suffering from post-traumatic stress disorder (PTSD). I never knew all this was abuse until I started counseling. I suffer from anxiety attacks now, which I am learning to control.

Within a couple of weeks after the incident, I got back my old job as an assistant manager! My boyfriend and I got married. We were working on supporting each other to stay sober. Everything was coming together slowly. Once we got to court, we had to come to an agreement on joint custody. This joint custody was probably one of the hardest things to go through because I would get phone calls from certain friends and family saying that my ex would be drinking and driving. I felt so scared that something bad would happen to them while they were out driving around. I felt helpless. When we went to court, the judge had warned us that if either of us got caught drinking or placing our son in any kind of danger, that parent would automatically lose custody. It took a close family member to finally call him in one day when he was drinking. I got a call to pick up my son and get another emergency custody for him. I had to stand in for my son because he was still a minor. It was probably the best feeling ever. That day, we finally returned to court and were granted full custody! I was excited. My ex had received a five-year restraining order on him: no contact with my son. I had received full custody! This was the happiest day of my life. I could raise my son in peace and safe out of harm's way.

With my brand-new life, new husband, and remaining sober, we were living a new life together. We also welcomed a new baby boy.

A few years later, I found myself becoming an advocate for other battered women. I have been able to help other women find the confidence they need to overcome their abuser by giving them the truth about their own strengths, being able to stand up to their spouse or significant others with words and not fists. I have seen women become scared and traumatized by what they went through (PTSD). Many endure physical abuse, and some don't make it out alive.

I have been able to help many of my coworkers, friends, and family in so many ways. I have opened up my home and let them in. Many women suffer from post-traumatic stress disorder (PTSD); I know I do. I have found strength in myself to look past my experience and help those in need. Domestic violence is something no one should ever go through. I want to educate women in toxic relationships and do so in a safer environment. I have opened my door many times and will do it again. You should not have to feel alone when someone is hurting you.

I realized my worth and know how I want to be treated. I want to make sure victims are safe. No one should ever have to lose their life at the hands of their abuser. Sad to say that many don't make it out alive because they think they can change them. When I finally walked away, I not only saved myself, but I saved him too. If either of us really hurt each other, one of us would be six feet under or behind bars. I've done things to him that I'm not proud of. I did not want to be in either place. I wanted to live. The way things were going between us, there's no telling where our lives would have been if I stayed. Who would be raising my son?

It's not worth trying to fix a toxic relationship when it's a one-sided love story. Narcissists are the worst to get into a relationship with. Don't rush a relationship; get to know one another. Look for red flags. The younger generation needs to be educated. Abuse is not okay.

Domestic Violence: Break the Silence.

BIOGRAPHY

Marisa Rico has taken part in a documentary about domestic violence. She was the first to help another advocate pursue the film. She has also created a private Facebook group called "You're Worth So Much!" empowering victims to take their power back. Her persistence and grit to serve others are so inspiring! Marisa has opened her home to victims and has counseled them. Marisa is creating a non-profit organization for victims. Marisa is life-proof, being an unstoppable and fearless leader with such a humble spirit. Marisa is proof that with enough determination, we all can transform our lives.

Connect with Marisa Rico via https://linktr.ee/Mkrico1980

CHAPTER 25

Never Again

By Aaron Rico

No parent should bury their children. I'll never be the same without him. What is precious to me is that I was there when he came into the world as a newborn, and I was there when he left—both times holding his hand. I will see him again. One day.

I grew up in an alcoholic family. My mom and stepfather were alcoholics. At first, it was only the weekends because they worked during the week. The binges usually started on Friday and lasted until Monday. Before I started drinking, my sister and I got accused of drinking beer. One Saturday afternoon, I confessed to drinking though I never did. But not long after that, the accusations of drinking their beer began again.

I thought to myself that I might as well find out what I'm getting beat for. I was eight years old when I took a drink for the first time. And through the years, I built up a tolerance, even going to elementary school buzzed. I just thought it was something people did, even though I didn't see other kids my age drinking.

My parents and uncle would let me drive their vehicles while I was sitting on their laps; I was nine years old. By junior high, I was tall enough to drive on my own. We would wake up early, and I would drive my mom to the bar that was fourteen miles out of town. She would buy the liquor (usually two cases of beer and two-fifths of whiskey). Then we'd return home. Mom would go inside, and I'd keep two six-packs in the backseat.

I would take the truck to school because they didn't want to go to jail for driving drunk.

Mom would shake so badly that she couldn't sign her personal checks, so she made me learn to forge her signature to buy more alcohol. It's how I sign my name to this day. I met my first wife at a party I threw at my house while my parents were both in rehab. She and I were still in high school. Eventually, my parents lost their jobs. We moved out of our house because my mom lost her job working for the government. We ended up moving into a one-room home with my stepfather's family. We had to get up at 4 a.m. every morning to catch the bus at 5 a.m. for school. I was in tenth grade at the time. I lived there for four weeks until I asked my girlfriend if I could move in with her family. It was a long shot, but her family agreed, and I moved back into town.

All this time, my drinking never slowed down. Finding ways to get drunk was easy. My sister moved in with her best friend and her family, and they took care of her. I will always be grateful for this. After graduating high school, mom was proud of me for enrolling in Junior College in Albuquerque. Parks College was 150 miles away. I enrolled in business and vowed no more drinking. I did okay, studied, made friends, and stayed sober.

I returned to my girlfriend's house during a semester break. My mom came by drunk. She was just happy for me and wanted to spend time with me because she missed me. I got angry and yelled at her, saying, "Don't come around here drunk. I don't want to see you when you're drunk!" And I never saw her again. Those were the last words I said to my mom.

I returned to school and my studies. On January 11, 1987, my world crashed. I vividly recall sitting in typing class when the dean of students sent her aide. It felt like high school; everyone was teasing me that I was going to see the principal. As I sat down in her office, she said quietly, "I have some bad news, Aaron. I don't have any way of telling you this, but your mother passed away early this morning." I tuned her out. I knew she was talking to me, but I was devastated. When I finally listened, she said someone from the tribe was coming by to take me home.

I went to my dorm room and closed the door. I just screamed! I felt so much emotion that I started trashing my room. I was out of control, so I started punching my armoire, harder and harder. I don't remember how many times I hit it, but my hand got so swollen. I opened the fridge, and there was my roommate's fifth of Jack Daniels. I started slamming it down. I finished it in an hour. I heard knocking at my door, and then keys opened it. The dean asked if I was alright. "No, my mom died," I said.

Two guys picked me up and took me to the junction at Smith Lake, where my aunties picked me up. I was drunk but not falling-down drunk. We stayed at my grandmother's house. On January 16, we laid my mom to rest. It was a cold morning. The people who helped with the burial couldn't dig the frozen ground. They had to get a backhoe to finish her grave. My biological father showed up at the funeral and took my sister and me to his favorite place in Gallup, Furr's Cafeteria. Later, we returned as it started snowing. We finally laid my mom to rest. I still miss my mom to this very day.

Her passing changed everything. For the rest of my life, it was work, partying, drinking hard, and then picking myself back up. Even when my first two kids were born, I wasn't much of a father. That's the greatest regret I have to this day. I wasn't there for them. My drink of choice—what do you got? I became so guilty about my life that I fell into a deep depression.

My girlfriend became my wife, and my firstborn was a son. Two years later, we had a daughter. But alcohol kept me away from them. Drinking made sure that my marriage didn't last long. Countless jobs were lost over the years, some really good jobs too. For so many years, it was just fights and accidents. I should have died so many times, but I believe my mom was my Guardian Angel and kept me safe.

I moved on to meet a girl in the mid-nineties. I don't exactly remember how I met her, but I liked her a lot. I tried staying sober while talking to her, but I needed a shot of courage. But I lost her due to my drinking. I thought I'd lost her forever, which drove me to drink even more. A year later, she walked into the store I was working at. I thought I'd never seen her again. She didn't even look at me. My heart jumped like crazy. I wanted her to look at me. Then I saw the black eye. It devastated me. I was angry and wanted to take her away. I saw her from time to time, gradually more often, and we eventually became friends again. One night, she told me she wanted out of the toxic relationship. I got scared, but it meant being with her again. I took the chance, but I paid the price by leaving my kids. She told me to tell them, but I didn't respond. In the long run, it really hurt them. I should have listened to her. But I was really happy that I was back in her life. We had our ups and downs. Our lowest points included jail and living homeless on the river. But the bright side was just being with her.

We came back to New Mexico in late 2006 to get things together. The night before we were supposed to return to Laughlin, her son and her ex came by her mom's place. There was a big fight about him drinking and driving with their son. We ended up taking her son in, and her ex-boyfriend drove off and wrecked his car. Unknowingly to us, that was the start of our life as a family. We got temporary custody. But we kept drinking, thinking that we could keep him and still drink. We almost lost custody of our son. I had to leave the family. I went to my uncle's house. I listened to him about changing my life. He had stopped drinking. His making that choice had a huge impact on my life. I just didn't know how yet.

My girlfriend came by my uncle's house. I thought I would never see her again. She talked to me about keeping her son, our relationship, and our future together and asked me to put the bottle down. She didn't want to lose her son again. I had given up alcohol before, but I always went back. I never thought about the consequences. But this time, it was for a purpose because I love her very much. So, I quit. Staying with her was the best decision I ever made. And I know that I would have never done it without her and our son in my life. She was my inspiration.

We made a decision on January 16, 2007: Never Again! We got married on May 23, 2007. My dream had come true. I couldn't believe it.

So many times, I'd tell others that I would never live past the age of forty. But I quit drinking when I was thirty-nine, and to this day, I'm amazed by my willpower and courage to give it up.

We did it cold turkey. I have never taken another drink since then. It wasn't easy in the beginning, but over time, saying "No" got easier. We also changed our lifestyle and friends. I'd quit so many times before, but I went back to drinking. And now, I just stopped. It has been over fourteen years of sobriety.

After years of guilt from the last words with my mom, I finally forgave myself for those words. Forgiving myself added to the purpose that helped me to stop drinking. It's weird that I can still taste the liquor when I'm standing at the checkout counter. But I still tell myself every day, "Not today. I'm never drinking again."

What hurts the most is that my oldest son died from drinking. I failed to help him with his drinking problem even though family and friends thought I could have. I just don't know what else I could have done to help him stop. We talked about it, but what made it harder for him to stop at the end was the loss of his mother a year earlier (also due to alcohol). During those last days, he repeatedly asked me about my mom, the pain I suffered when she passed, and how I survived the guilt and emptiness.

No parent should bury their children. I'll never be the same without him. What is precious to me is that I was there when he came into the world as a newborn, and I was there when he left—both times holding his hand. I will see him again . . . one day.

My son told me before he passed, "Dad, you're the strongest person I know." But I have never thought of myself as "strong." Changing your life and your habits comes down to forgiving yourself, loving others, and living for a purpose bigger than yourself.

Every day I thank God for what he has given to me. I'm better now, fourteen plus years of sobriety, after thirty years of drinking hard liquor. I'm blessed in so many ways. I still have my health, mind, and spirit. And I'm blessed with my wife. I love her. She's been there for me more than I can thank her for. She is my life. We've got to be strong to raise our four boys.

BIOGRAPHY

Aaron Rico's determination to quit drinking alcohol has inspired others to quit drinking. The loss of his son gave him the willpower to keep living life with his family. He has shared his story with others suffering from alcohol addiction. He has done this with no counseling and rehabilitation help and services.

CHAPTER 26

The Power Of *One* Decision

By Michelle Archer Momeny

The phone call felt like it came from hell: "There has been a shooting at your husband's work!" My blood ran cold, and my mouth was instantly devoid of all saliva. I could hear my heart beating out of my chest and the blood rushing in my ears, and I started shaking uncontrollably. I don't know how, but I *knew* deep in my heart that it was him. It was Ryan, my husband of thirteen years.

My co-worker drove me to his facility, and we were met with news choppers, police cars, crime scene tape, and throngs of evacuated workers forced out of the surrounding buildings. I was forced to wait, just like everyone else. I was screaming at the police officer that I had to find out. I had to know if it was him. He replied that I would have to wait until the detective got there. The detective finally arrived and walked me to his SUV. He made me sit inside, introduced me to some on-site trauma response counselors, and said he would be right back.

He asked what my husband was wearing that day. I said I wasn't sure, but since his team, the Seattle Seahawks, had won their first Super Bowl in franchise history yesterday, I would assume it was a Seahawks jersey and jeans. He then confirmed that it was him. He was dead from multiple gunshot wounds.

My Ryan, the love of my life, was gone forever at the hands of a co-worker. That was February 3, 2014. I was forty-four years old and now, a sudden widow.

Time seemed to stop. I mechanically ran through all the post-death tasks I had to deal with. I was surrounded by people making promises that they would never keep. Their world continued to spin and move forward, and this became a distant memory of something that happened to other people. It didn't affect them as much anymore, and they couldn't figure out why I was still clenched in the claws of grief, anxiety, PTSD, and overwhelming sadness. I was literally living in the movie *Groundhog Day*. I relived that day repeatedly for years, and it triggered panic attacks and an emotional shutdown.

For the next five years, I would stuff down emotions, be "strong," go to work, and be a high achiever as usual. But inside, I was anything but normal. I was suffering from stomach aches, nausea, headaches, depression, and reclusiveness. Coming home to an empty house, I would sit in my closet and cry from the deepest guttural part of my being. I stopped caring about myself. I was going through the motions of existing. I was stuck between hating the way I felt every day and the guilt of what it meant to move on. Would I be forced to forget him and the years we spent together and erase him completely from my memory to heal from the pain? That didn't feel right. I didn't want to move on. What in the hell was I moving on *from*? I didn't choose this. I was forced into this.

One day, I woke up, looked up to heaven, and said to Ryan, "I know you are so disappointed in me right now. I have let myself go, and I have no motivation for anything in life."

I heard his voice clearly say to me, "I'm sorry you are hurting. Just know that I am here every day in your heart and that it is okay to take steps to heal. You don't have to forget me, but you do need to love yourself enough to thrive. You have half of your life left to live, and you can make a difference in people's lives with your story. I have no doubt you can do this."

Later that day, I went for a walk with the dogs, and an eagle landed on a tree on the side of the lake close to me. I had seen an eagle right after Ryan was murdered, and I knew that was his spirit animal. So, to see that eagle after my "conversation" with him, I knew I would be okay and that I would be guided through my next steps.

In order to allow and follow this intuitive guidance, I had to get out of my own way. I knew I had to be a part of something bigger than myself that would make a difference in others' lives and honor the life of my lost love.

Having been an avid fitness and nutrition enthusiast my entire life, I felt a calling back to it. I started practicing self-care with yoga, meditation, meditative walks, and barre workouts. Since I felt less nauseous, I started eating again. I began to feel so much clearer. Stepping out of my comfort zone, I found myself saying hi to other people in my class (I'm sure introverts can relate to this difficulty). I met other widows who had been exercising alongside me, and I never knew their story until I allowed myself to open up to them.

I learned about the power of community. I relearned the power of mindfulness and self-love. I relearned that the body and mind are powerfully connected, and we have the innate ability to heal ourselves. I learned there is no such thing as "moving on." It is about "moving through"—moving through the pain of grief to allow love to remain and guide your heart.

My heart was leading me to help others who have faced loss and are stuck in their pain and grief. I was unsure of what it would look like, but I trusted my intuition and spirit guide. That intuition led me to complete my 200-hour yoga teacher certification, a Level 2 Grief Yoga⬚ teacher certification, thirty hours of somatic therapy training, in-depth training on relationships, connection, and authentic heart-centered marketing. I also joined a network marketing business. Initially, it was to force me out of my comfort zone once again and enjoy a discount on the amazing nutrition products, but what I got in return was a massive set of self-development tools and training, a newfound sense of support and community, a new best friend, and a new path to self-healing.

I have connected with mentors and feel that my journey of personal development is in its infant stages. I feel like I have created an amazing foundation for myself, which helps me be the go-to person for assisting others to holistically heal and move through their grief using movement, sound, breath, and nutrition.

I'm sure you are thinking to yourself, 'Well, that is great and may work for you, but I can never do what you did. I'm too *'insert adjective.'* Guess what? I never thought I could do it either. What I *do* know is that by intentionally doing this *one* thing every day, I could redesign my future.

That one thing is **The Power of *One* Decision**.

It looks like this.

Every morning when I wake up, I make a decision that today I will do *one* thing that will help *one* person. That one person can be me or someone else. If I find myself self-sabotaging my efforts by turning off the alarm clock, crying into my pillow, or spending all day unshowered and in my PJs, I ask myself, "What would Ryan think of that decision?" and "Whose life will I impact today by just schlepping around my house?"

I read and re-read the book, *The 5-Second Rule*, by Mel Robbin. The 5-Second Rule is simple: ***If you have an instinct to act on something, you must physically move within five seconds, or your brain will kill it.***

Combining that with **The Power of *One* Decision** is a game-changer.

Yes, we still need to grieve.

Yes, we still need to mourn.

However, there comes the point in time when your body and health start to get affected by grief if it is not dealt with and expressed adequately. There is no *one* way to grieve. Everyone's grief journey is very different. Grief can follow the death of a loved one or a child, the loss of a marriage, the loss of a job, or the loss of a friendship. It doesn't necessarily revolve around just death.

The one common thing that occurs when grief and pain are not expressed, and when we hold it in (because people think we should be "over it by now" and we don't want to "bug" people with our grief), is its manifestation in the body tissues. This is where the quote, "The issues are in the tissues," comes from. Our bodies get stuck in the state of "Fight-

or-Flight," which is the oldest part of the brain (the reptilian brain) that keeps us alive and safe when faced with danger. When our bodies are stuck in that state, cortisol and adrenaline are the main hormones being constantly pumped through the body.

In the book, *The Body Keeps the Score*, by Bessel Van Der Kolk, MD, the author describes the effects of the elevated fight-or-flight hormones as increased heart rate and blood pressure, which puts a strain on the heart and other body systems. Under normal conditions, the body can turn the stress hormones on and off quickly and take us to a place of rest and digest (a calm state). Those who have faced trauma or emotional stress have higher levels of stress hormones flooding their bloodstream, and it takes longer to "turn off." The long-term effects of this include issues with memory, attention span, irritability, sleep problems, muscle aches, stomach issues, and more. Over time, many serious and long-term health issues can occur.

As someone who suffers from anxiety and PTSD from that horrific day, I was eager to learn how to turn off those fight-or-flight hormones that were eating me alive. Using holistic healing methods such as yoga asana, meditation, pranayama (breath), mindfulness, and sound expression to stimulate the vagus nerve, we can aid and retrain our nervous system. I call it "Emotional Healing."

Here is the thing. You can spend all the time you have left in this world feeling sad, anxious, depressed, alone, or whatever your particular feeling is, *or* you can make *one* decision every single day that will move the needle forward through your grief and emotions.

After talking with many widows, here are a few things that I have witnessed:

- Rumination: They can't imagine living life without their person.
- Depression: What is the point of living?
- Sadness: It has been three years, and I cry every day.
- Isolation: I am so lonely.
- Shame: I have gained so much weight.

- Guilt: I wasn't there for them when they died.

- PTSD: I replay that day over and over in my head like it just happened, and I feel the same emotional triggers.

- Anxious: I'm so stressed about money. Will my kids be okay? How can I live this life without my partner?

Maybe we were raised in a challenging environment. Maybe we suffer from a lack of self-belief. We may have never learned proper stress recovery or coping skills. We may have never witnessed a loss or been able to express our emotions. We may have never learned that the mind-body connection is so powerful. We may have never learned proper nutrition and the body's needs for it to thrive.

What it boils down to is this:

- It is never too late to learn something new.

- You are never so broken that you can't heal.

- You will never dishonor your lost love by creating a new and fulfilling life. In fact, they would be damn proud of you!

Even if you have never practiced self-care or self-love, it is time to start. *Because* the body has an innate ability to heal itself, all it needs is some loving input and daily intentional action from you.

Through my trauma, I'm grateful that I have found a way to help others by blending the skills I have learned around holistic healing and network marketing. This allows me to offer others various choices along their path of healing to improve their life and health, gain emotional and financial security, and be a part of a supportive community.

BIOGRAPHY

Michelle Archer Momeny is an Oregon-based Clinical Laboratory Scientist of thirty years, specializing in Microbiology (BS, MT, ASCP), a registered RYS 200 Yoga Teacher, and a Level 2 Registered Grief Yoga® Instructor with forty hours of Somatic Yoga Therapy training. She lost her husband to a workplace shooting in 2014 and was sucked into the vortex of grief, PTSD, anxiety, and panic. Michelle has been a lifelong student of fitness, nutrition, personal development, and the mind-body/science connection. Tired of feeling stuck in grief, she became a student of holistic emotional healing that embodies movement, breath, and sound to move grief through the body. She is building a home-based business as well as training and empowering others to be able to create emotional and financial security for themselves and their families, all while being supported in a thriving community. You can learn more about Michelle and her offerings on her website https://theempoweredwidow.com/

Connect with Michelle Archer Momeny via https://mich23.link/

CHAPTER 27

Out Of The Darkness, Into The Light

By Regina Ruiz

I believe we all tend to have a secret very few people, if any, know about. This is one event in my life I have not shared with many people.

I was raised in a home where abuse was normal. Although we had food, shelter, and clothing, something was lacking. That something was love and a true family relationship. Love to me was providing material things to survive, but a true connection and a loving, healthy relationship were not provided. I have never known a true father's love.

Growing up with five siblings in a single-story, three-bedroom home made for a very close, cozy family unit. There were four boys in one bedroom, two girls in the other. We all had to share one bathroom. I was quite fortunate to have only one roommate. The age difference between my sister and me made it a little bit easier, as she had left home after a while, and I had the room to myself. The same can be said of our oldest brother.

Having a former military man for a father made for a very militant lifestyle. We endured the upending of the beds if they were not made up to standard, the dumping of dresser drawers if they were messy, and the white glove treatment along the tops of the door frames. Any dust or dirt found had to be corrected and ASAP! Everything had to be done before we could enjoy our breakfast. Eating around our father was another story. I had become an anxious eater and tended to be on the skinnier side since it was so difficult to eat around him. At that time and age, I was unaware of these symptoms; abuse is real, and its effects have names.

I have always believed myself to be a strong person, but I didn't realize how dangerous my situation was at that age.

I'm sharing this snippet of my childhood to continue with my story—my secret I have shared with hardly anyone.

After I was a little older, I thought that I'd be able to handle myself around my father, and things would get better. I met someone, thought I fell in love and agreed to marry him. I was eighteen at the time, and I knew everything . . . or so I thought! My controlling father was adamant that I was not to marry him and did everything in his power to prevent it. I thought I was in love and didn't really understand what marriage was supposed to be. This man was my first everything, love, lover, and soon-to-be husband. I've never really had a relationship with a man, and the only thing I could compare it to was my relationship with my father. I just didn't know what I was getting myself into at the time. All I knew was I wanted to marry this man and start a life away from home. I failed to mention this man was three years older than me. He was worldly, a bad boy, and mature!

Being raised a Catholic, I was quite programmed to believe that I would go to hell if I sinned and did not repent. Knowing I had relations with this man, I felt I was obligated to marry him. As you can see, my upbringing and my beliefs at the time made for a very messed up start to my adult life. There were so many events that happened which led me to this story. I feel I need to share. I had an abusive childhood, a religious upbringing, and held the belief that I had to be okay and accept what was happening to me, feeling I deserved it. The way my father was raising my siblings and me seemed like such an oxymoron. But at the time, we believed that's how it was: strict religious rules, abuse, an iron fist, and lots of chores.

Married life seemed wonderful! My husband had a good job. We got along very well, and I did everything in my power to please him. I created a warm, clean, and welcoming home. Thanks to all the chores

I alluded to earlier, I was an excellent cook, so dinner was on the table every night, and I tried to make sure he was also pleased in the bedroom, considering I was very limited in my experience.

All seemed to be going well for the first few months, at least I thought so. All of this was new to me: a home, a husband, and all the responsibilities that came with it. But then, it seemed that after only around six months, things started to change. My husband would start coming home later, and later, dinner got cold, and I got tired of waiting for him every night. Never a phone call nor an apology. I put up with it since that is what marriage is all about, right? It didn't happen every night at first, but it happened often enough that I was getting concerned. I wanted to start a family with this man, and he couldn't even be courteous enough to come home every night to his wife and dinner. Soon, he would even stay gone overnight.

I thought if we talked about things, we could fix it. If I could get pregnant, I could fix it. After trying and trying to get pregnant, I failed. I blamed myself. Since my self-esteem was low enough, why not? Why wouldn't it be my fault? I was never on birth control, I never had other partners, but I still blamed myself. I was never made aware of the fact that since I was sexually active, I was supposed to have a female checkup. I never experienced that either. I was scared, but I was determined to find out what was wrong with me. Why couldn't I get pregnant? I made the appointment, and as it got closer, I was getting more and more anxious and scared. I didn't know what to expect. I asked my husband to go with me. He laughed and said, "No way!" I had to go alone. It was painful and humiliating, but I endured it. After consulting with the doctor, it was determined that it was not my fault. Everything was okay on my end. I was told to just relax and stop being so anxious, and it would happen. After two and a half years, it never happened.

I endured the lack of making a baby and having a husband who didn't want to come home to me. I felt I had failed all aspects of my life. I made a terrible wife, and I couldn't even produce a child. I have always wanted children, and I couldn't even do that right. I was so depressed and sad all the time. I called my sister one night and told her I was worthless and done with life. I had swallowed a lot of pills. The only way she knew I was serious was because of my slurring voice.

She rushed over and took me to the ER. My stomach was pumped, and I was going to be alright. I hadn't taken enough to end it all, apparently. I couldn't even do that right. Back then, there was no counseling to find out why I did it and if I was going to try it again. I knew I wouldn't because I realized I was still there for a reason. I didn't know why at the time, and I wouldn't know for a long time.

If it weren't for the love and support of my sister, I would no longer be on this earth. I don't think my mom even knew I had attempted suicide. I hoped she didn't so she wouldn't be disappointed with me. I survived because there was at least *one* person here who didn't want me to die. She wanted to love me and have me in her life for as long as possible. Today, I have two beautiful adult children and three adorable grandsons. These lives would not be here today if I had succeeded in my suicide attempt. I believe I have touched many lives, not by telling my story but by being living proof that there is nothing so bad in your life that it needs to end in suicide.

A short time later, my sister introduced me to Jesus Christ. That is another story for another time.

BIOGRAPHY

Regina Ruiz's career focus has been on training and quality. Helping others is her life's passion, so training employees to become the best has been the highlight of her career. As a single mother, she has faced many challenges and has overcome many to become who she is today. With a passion for being a servant leader, she spends her spare time volunteering and donating money to her favorite charities. Regina enjoys life with her two adult children and three grandsons.

Connect with Regina Ruiz via https://linktr.ee/reginaruiz777

CHAPTER 28

Surviving By God's Grace Through The Love Of My Family

By Sahar Naghshi

"When all the dust is settled and all the crowds are gone,
the things that matter are faith, family and friends!"[24]
—Barbara Bush

I know that family is not everything, but mine means a lot to me. They are the foundation of my life. I have always felt blessed to be around my loved ones. Then, there are friends we meet along the way who become family by way of hearts! Those friends stay with us forever no matter what. As Barbara Bush expressed in the above quote, the things that matter for me are faith, family, and friends!

In 1979, in a small city called Sardasht, a Kurdish family of four was just welcoming their fifth member: the third child, a little sister, who her auntie named Sahar. Little did she know that she was born right after the Iranian Revolution in a country with extreme political and religious turbulence. Not to mention a new government, far from any kind of that decade's government—an out-of-ordinary government. This was

---

24 Pat Ralph, "12 Quotes That Show Why Barbara Bush Was Such a Beloved First Lady," Business Insider, April 18, 2018, https://www.businessinsider. in/12-quotes-that-show-why-barbara-bush-was-such-a-beloved-first-lady/ articleshow/63818962.cms.

a government based on sharia—God's government! In 1979, the new prime minister, Ayatollah Khomeini, appointed opposition leader Mehdi Bazargan as his own prime minister and commanded Iranians to obey Bazargan as a religious duty.

'A government based on sharia is God's government' is what we were told. In other words, opposing the government meant opposing the sharia of Islam. Revolt against God's government was a revolt against God. Revolt against God was blasphemy.

There comes a time in life when one must stand firm and say, 'No!'

To make that story about a hell of a revolution short, let me share the after-effects it had on us Kurdish people and many other ethnicities and non-Islamic people. We had to say goodbye to liberty, democracy, peace, freedom of expression, and freedom of religion. We also had to part with several basic human rights, such as reading and writing in our first language and wearing our own national dress. To this day, I still wonder how it was possible to be born in a place and not have the right to live and grow in that place. I say this because where I grew up, if you simply expressed your opinion about your basic rights as a human being, you'd be executed!

How could we just stay silent and accept such a dictatorial government?! Fortunately, my dad, my hero, didn't just sit there doing nothing. At the time, he was a freedom and liberty activist. He, along with several thousands of Kurdish men and women, stood together and said, 'No! We cannot tolerate being stripped of our human rights.'

That is where our journey to escape the country began. My dad decided to move out of the city, and later, out of the country, following his dream to fight for the freedom of his people. So, there we went: my mum with her three kids, the youngest one (me, just eight months old), my sister (three years old), and my big brother (five and a half years old), riding on horses, moving through the villages near the borders of Iraq, through a perilous and turbulent time with several domestic wars. My mum tells me how we had to stop and stay in different villages and then move forward to a new village to survive. While we were riding, we had to stop and hide in the mountains because the helicopters would be just above us and would bombard the area. Unsure of whether we would survive, and living with so much fear, we were taken on a hell of a ride!

To make a long story short, after living in the different villages near the borders of Iraq for three years, with my dad secretly working with all the other freedom activists in the mountains of Kurdistan, we moved to the southern part of Kurdistan in Iraq (under Saddam's regime at the time). By that time, my oldest brother moved back to Sardasht to live with our grandmother's family, and he grew up there without us.

After moving out of the borders of Iran, we welcomed the fourth member of our family: a little brother. We lived in a very small city named Qala Cholan. After a couple of months of residing there, we moved to another city because of another domestic war. That is when we moved to Suleimania: a big and beautiful city in the southern part of Kurdistan. This is where I started primary school. We lived there for three years, and then we had to move again because my dad got another work project in a little village near to the Qandil Mountains.

So we ended up living in this beautiful fairytale village called Enze. Enze was a beautiful village with high mountains, forests, waterfalls, and lakes. That is where I experienced most of my beautiful childhood memories. After a couple of years in Enze, we welcomed the fifth member of our family, another little brother, who is now a young and wise thirty-year-old man. Being a domestic war zone, it was not always safe to live there. Eventually, the Iranian military forces bombarded the village. Again, we had to move, leaving our home behind. It was not only us but thousands of other Kurdish families and freedom activists who fought for peace and liberty (the Kurdish-Iranian Political Party).

We survived several wars, moving from city to city, village to village, through the southern part of Kurdistan. I truly believe that we made it so far by God's grace. To go beyond survival and save our lives, our family made the final decision: move out of Kurdistan for good. I still remember that day as clear as crystal. My grandfather came to visit us all the way from Iran, and my mother's aunt from Canada.

Moving forward was the only way to survive.

My dad's life was in danger. Many of his co-workers were terrorized on their way to work in Iraq, and we were no longer safe. Our future was also very insecure! My parents considered moving out of the country to save their children's lives and secure our future.

This journey of freedom became a journey of survival. To save our country from a dictator's regime, dad had to save his children first—the next generation of Kurds. They would eventually fight for the freedom of Kurdistan, not by war but by knowledge, peace, and negotiations.

So, there we went again, with a suitcase, almost no money, and some pieces of gold which my mum had to sell to get us passports. Now we were on the road again, to the next destination—a destination where we could make our dream of freedom come true. After waiting in the checking queue for an entire day in the heat of mid-summer in June 1994, near the borders of Turkey, in the city of Zakho, we eventually went through and passed the border of Turkey late at night.

That was one of the longest trips of my life. After approximately twenty-six hours by bus, we arrived at Ankara, the capital of Turkey. And then, we had to go through the UN's legalities and procedures for Turkey so we could move on to the next chapter of our lives. After one week of living in a small, dirty, rented room alongside another Kurdish family and having to go to the UN office almost every day to find out what was happening, the UN finally accepted ours as a refugee case. Then, we moved to another city by train, where my dad had several Kurdish contacts assist us in finding an abode until we were transited to another country for good. After a couple of weeks, my oldest brother also moved to Turkey from Kurdistan. After arriving in Kayseri and settling down temporarily, my older sister and I dreamed of going back to school every time we saw all the other kids go to school in their uniform. To survive two long years in Turkey, my siblings and I had to work for a living. After approximately two years of waiting, we got a message that we would be transiting to Norway. And finally, we got here!

I know I just had to keep going no matter what. In my personal life, I have fallen many times: getting a divorce and failing two network marketing businesses. Still, I had to get up and take the next step to move forward. Moving forward is the only way we can succeed in reaching our dreams!

So now, arriving in a third country, with all its challenges (not knowing the language and the culture), we started from scratch. I still remember the first year. I kept going to school just to learn the language and improve myself every day so that I could start college. I felt very lonely in school, and it was difficult to make new friends because we had nothing in common: neither a shared history nor childhood. The eagerness to learn the language kept me going to school every day till I managed to get into college.

In the meantime, my sister wanted to marry her lover, who ended up in the other part of the world: Australia. She would soon move to Australia. I was happy for her but sad at the same time. Of course, I was sad. Only God knew when I would see her again. It was not easy going back to school without my sister. It felt like I lost a very important person in my life. I really look up to my sister. She is not only my sibling but also my best friend, my soul mate, and my supervisor in life. Not having my sister, studying by means of another language in which I needed daily improvement, and facing a host of other challenges, I had to work thrice as hard to make it through all the exams. I eventually made it through and got into university.

Then, the journey of studying began. I had to work at the same time to survive financially, and I did. My studies took me much longer than expected because I had to change directions to figure out what I wanted to study. In the end, I studied early childhood teaching and got my bachelor's degree, and now, I have worked as a pedagogy leader in kindergarten for the past ten years.

I was inspired by the lives of those who survived the war!

Yes, my life has been a battle of surviving. At the end of the day, all the suffering of living in the century of war and survival has taught me the true meaning of life: Be grateful for still being alive and being surrounded by your loved ones.

Surviving war has been an excellent training process for me. Were it not so brutal, I would recommend it as an "Intro to Life 101" course. Years of hard work, endurance, determination, conviction, and fighting for the right to stay alive and free and be ourselves has given us the will to move mountains.

Let's move mountains together! If I can do that, you surely can!

BIOGRAPHY

Sahar Naghshi is a living example of surviving war with her family, which she had to do several times. Through those life experiences, she has not only found the true meaning of life but also the golden nuggets of how to start from scratch and still be able to move mountains. Her career as an early childhood teacher is about inspiring and helping others. In her case, it's about helping children grow and become the best version of themselves. She is very passionate about helping, supporting, and guiding parents to a more positive upbringing of their children. She also runs two successful network marketing businesses from home alongside her daily job to pursue her dreams and to help everyday people reach their goals and dreams. With the help of this book, she hopes to inspire others to find their true meaning in life and never give up on their dreams, no matter what the circumstances. Now she is living in the south-eastern part of Norway with her only child and her husband. She is dedicated to her family and her work as a childcare teacher.

Connect with Sahar Naghshi via https://linktr.ee/MPnm

CHAPTER 29

Creating Life Balance Through Three-Dimensional Fitness

By Dr. Tasheema Fair

What is three-dimensional fitness? It is a combination of spiritual, mental, and physical fitness. I am a firm believer that everyone is a spirit, that they have a soul and live in a body. It means you are a three-part being. To be fit, you must practice fitness with each part of yourself so as to create a balanced life. Most people are unaware of three-dimensional fitness, or they fail to practice it.

Most people may practice one or two parts of three-dimensional fitness, but they never gain balance in their lives. For instance, you can be very disciplined in physical fitness but fail to practice mental fitness and be super depressed. A person can be very spiritual, but their physical health may be poor because they neglect to practice physical fitness. To be honest, there have been times when I did not practice three-dimensional fitness, and my life went out of balance. I learned that in order to disrupt the chaos, I must take care of *all* of myself. This is not taught in grade school, college, or medical school. It is a life lesson.

Let us talk about spiritual fitness. It means different things depending on your culture and who you worship. As a spiritual being, you should stay connected to the Source from which you came. As for me and my house, we worship God. He is my source. The way I stay connected to God is by being in constant communication with Him daily. I believe in the power of prayer. I read my Bible so that I can learn how to deal with the everyday hustle of life. It is also important for me to worship corporately with other believers when I can. When I'm not traveling or working, I make it a point to go to church. I would argue that spiritual fitness is the most critical aspect of fitness.

There were times when everything would come apart, and nothing apart from my connection to God could help me. For example, back in 2011, my father passed away while I was deployed. I was lost. I was numb and disconnected from reality. No self-help books or personal development could help me put things into perspective. Exercise and nutrition did not help because I barely ate, and when I was able to exercise, the pain only subsided for a little bit. I was back in despair. Nothing helped me process his death in a healthy way. I was broken. I knew God was my only way out. I focused almost entirely on my spiritual fitness. When I was angry, I prayed. When I was sad, I prayed. When I was lonely, I prayed. I knew that was the only way I was going to heal from the trauma. It took time to heal. It took a lot of prayers and just talking to God. It took people praying for me and with me. As I healed, I was able to work on my mental fitness and get back to healthy living.

Let us switch gears and talk about mental fitness. Mental fitness is being cognizant of what you hear, what you see, and what you say. The things we hear in the news, what we watch on TV and social media, and what we say about ourselves can affect us mentally. Mental fitness is being resilient, even when life is not going so well. It is the ability to bounce back from adversity. The famous speaker, Les Brown, says, "If you fall, fall on your back. If you can look up, you can get up."[25]

Negative stimuli and negative thinking are all around us, but it is important to counter-attack those thoughts with positivity everyday. Therefore, personal and professional development is so important. Personal development helps you eliminate as much negative stimuli as possible to protect your mental status. Listening to podcasts that focus on having a better mindset, reading self-help books, and saying things about

---

25 "Les Brown Quotes," BrainyQuote (Xplore), accessed July 23, 2021, https://www.brainyquote.com/quotes/les_brown_389885.

yourself that build you up are all part of practicing mental fitness. I'm sure you know the saying "train your brain or remain the same." Your brain is a muscle, and you must train it like you train your skeletal muscles. Now, you cannot lift weights with your brain, but you can pick up a book like this one and read it. Training your brain gives you clarity, helps you to develop better habits, makes you more productive, and reduces stress.

During my first year of medical school, I had adversity attacking me from every angle. That was the year 9/11 happened, and I was super stressed out from working and studying all the time. My first semester went well, but during my second semester, I began to crash. Even before I became a soldier, I had this innate ability to soldier up, but that was not always the right thing to do. I was failing my genetics class. School was taking its toll on me, and I wanted to quit. Spiritually and physically, I was okay, but mentally, I was going downhill. All I did was work, study, and workout. It was a vicious cycle. I am not saying that it's wrong to focus on your work. However, if you do not have any balance in your life, you become a robot. That is not the way we were created. I neither took a break to gather my thoughts nor did I take time to read anything else except for my medical books. I never took any time to relax.

During spring break, I went home to my parents. I told my mother I wanted to quit. She would not let me do that, and we went to talk to my pastor. I had a counseling session with Pastor Teri Crider. I cried and told her what was happening, and she listened intently. When I was done, she told me that I needed to chill out. I was stressing myself out over nothing. I needed to believe in my ability to pass my classes. She told me to watch a good comedy movie and relax. On that day I learned that I needed to give myself more grace. I needed to take control over my thoughts. I learned that it's okay to expect more from myself, but I should never beat myself up when things don't turn out the way I planned. I had to clear out any negative thoughts that told me I was defeated. There was a plan for my life, and I had to see it to fruition. For that, I needed balance.

We all know about physical fitness and how important it is to move our bodies. We will talk about exercise in this part of the chapter.

Remember that physical fitness is only part of the equation. The most important part is nutrition. What we eat dramatically affects our mood, how we feel about ourselves, and how much energy we have. Food is the fuel that gives our bodies the energy it needs to perform, down to the cellular level. Essentially, you are what you eat. Are you fueling your body with premium nutrients or processed food that makes you sluggish and slow?

Your body needs so many calories to function, and that need is based on the individual. Your body also needs the right amount of macronutrients (carbs, healthy fats, and protein) and micronutrients (vitamins and minerals) to perform well. In terms of weight management, everyone has a different journey. One lifestyle modification is not superior to the other. You need to switch over to a lifestyle that keeps your metabolism firing—a lifestyle with which you get all the nutrients you need. Diets do not work; they kill your metabolism. You may see some initial results, but when you stop or start to plateau, you become discouraged and gain the weight back. Eat to keep your body as efficient as possible.

Exercise is twenty percent of the equation. Movement is important to strengthen your muscles, joints, and bones. Movement is also great for all your organs, especially the heart. The American Heart Association says that we need 150 minutes of exercise per week to maintain cardiovascular health. That is five times a week for thirty minutes a day.[26] The kind of movement you do depends on how you want to look. If you want to look toned, then you do more high-intensity workouts and resistance training. I would argue we all should be doing some form of resistance training to strengthen our muscles and bones. Ladies, hear me out. It is okay to do resistance training. You will not look bulky unless you are eating more and lifting heavy weights. Cardio, resistance training, and eating clean will help you burn fat.

---

26 "Heart Health at Any Age – 40, 50, 60 and Beyond," American Heart Association, accessed July 23, 2021, https://www.heart.org/en/news/2018/07/20/heart-health-at-any-age-40-50-60-and-beyond.

I went through my own physical health journey, and I still am on it. It is a lifelong journey. I was heavy-set as a young girl, but as I got older, I knew I needed to be at a healthy weight. So, I tried different fad diets, pills, potions, etc. None of these gave me any real, lasting results. I discovered the right way to eat that suited my needs. I lost forty pounds in six months and gained more energy than ever before. No, it was not easy, but it was simple. I made some small changes in my nutrition, and I was able to accomplish my goal. I also learned to celebrate every small win throughout my journey to motivate myself. I teach my clients to do the same.

As you can see, creating more balance requires you to work on all of yourself. You must be disciplined in the practice of three-dimensional fitness. If something is out of order, that should alert you to see where you are slacking. Focus on the area that needs the most work until it catches up to the others.

Remember to not take the other two aspects of fitness for granted, as they are all connected. I encourage you to start practicing this concept, as it will drastically change your life for the better.

BIOGRAPHY

Dr. Tasheema Fair is a board-certified Obstetrician/Gynecologist, Health and Wellness Coach, and an LTC in the United States Army Reserves. She is the recent author of *Creating Life Balance With The Power of 3-Dimensional Fitness*. She is an entrepreneur in the network marketing industry and uses her skills as a physician to help women live healthier and happier lives by creating the lives that they desire. As a health coach, Dr. Fair helps professional women who struggle with weight loss to lose weight and keep it off. For more information about Dr. Fair's coaching and mentorship services, please visit www.ladydocnutrition.com.

Connect with Dr. Tasheema Fair via https://linktr.ee/Ladydocfit78

CHAPTER 30

What Drives Me To Success

By Vineet Bhardwaj

It was June 21, 2001. My good friend was in town from Miami. So, we headed out that night and hit the dance clubs in downtown Chicago, which was about fifty miles northwest of where my friend and I grew up. Few months before that, I was suffering from awful headaches and couldn't figure out why. That day, I was looking at one of the clubs' business cards, and it looked blurry when I tried to read it. I found this to be really strange because, since childhood, my vision was always better than 20/20. I was thirty years old at the time. So, I thought to myself, 'I just need glasses since I'm getting older.' I went to my local LensCrafters to get an eye exam and a pair of glasses. During the exam, the doctor said what I was saying wasn't making any sense! I was able to see certain things, but not others! So, I was sent straight to the emergency room at Central Dupage Hospital, which was about fifteen minutes away. They took my blood pressure when I got there, and it was 223/137. It turned out that I had been suffering from a kidney disease for seven to ten years, and now, I had end-stage renal disease (ESRD), which meant there was no hope to save them, and I had to either be on dialysis or get a kidney transplant. So, I stayed in the hospital for five days! During those five days, I was on dialysis, and when I first came into the hospital, I was 160 pounds. After five days of dialysis, I was 140 pounds, which means I had twenty pounds of toxins in my body!! That explained a lot.

Most people would have been upset and devastated, but quite honestly, I was relieved. Why? Because deep down inside, I knew there was something wrong with me, but I couldn't figure out what it was. For many, many years, I was fatigued, suffering from headaches, and could barely function daily to the point where I stopped living a normal life. I was having trouble in college when I was attending Northern Illinois (during ages eighteen to twenty-one) because, looking back, my body and brain were exhausted. But I thought it was psychological; I thought the symptoms were due to depression because I flunked out of college twice, and my relationships with people were not going as planned. Another part of me thought maybe I was simply lazy. But that couldn't have been the case because I was working full-time at a temp agency when I was diagnosed. I also worked part-time bartending at Olive Garden and going to Columbia College part-time for fiction writing so I could publish children's books. The doctors couldn't believe I was doing all that while having ESRD. Honestly, I couldn't believe it either. Looking back, I was just a zombie, going through the motions. A few months later, my numbers got so bad I had to go on dialysis. I was waiting for a kidney transplant because my brother was a perfect match, but we had to wait for one year. Why?

So, here's the second part of the story. Around the same time I was diagnosed with ESRD, my younger brother (by four years) was diagnosed with bipolar disorder, and we had to make sure his meds wouldn't complicate the transplant. We finally got the okay, and on October 01, 2002, on my brother's twenty-seventh birthday, I got my transplant. After that, everything seemed to be getting better. I had my kidney, my brother was getting the help he needed with his bipolar, and we were back to normal life (as normal as it could get). Unfortunately, the worst was yet to come.

On September 24, 2007, my brother had been off his meds for about a week, pulled out of our driveway in his Firehawk, sped away, lost control of the car, and hit our neighbor's tree, three houses down. He was in a coma, and the doctors did not expect him to make it. Luckily, he came out of the coma three days later. But after that, he wasn't just bipolar, he had a permanent traumatic brain injury (a fourth-grader's math skills and a second-grader's reading skills), and the accident caused him to become schizophrenic as well. This brought a new challenge to our family.

Two years later, my kidney, which was supposed to last twenty to thirty years, failed after just seven years. At first, they thought the kidney failure was due to my strep throat in college and that it ate away at my kidneys over the years. But after it failed again so quickly, they found out I actually suffer from a very rare disease called IgA nephropathy. That's where your own immune system attacks your kidneys. So, every time I have a transplant, my immune system will eventually discover it and attack it! I was back to dialysis, and I did what was called peritoneal dialysis, where you have a catheter attached to your belly and carry out the dialysis at home. I would connect the catcher to a bag filled with fluid. The fluid would sit in my stomach for two hours, and then, I'd let it drain into an empty bag. I would have to do this five times a day. Then, over the course of four years, I got three major stomach infections because the catheter got contaminated and destroyed my peritoneal cavity and stomach lining, causing me to lose twenty-five pounds. I was underweight and could only eat about one and a half meals a day. Anything more and I'd vomit.

This has been going on since 2013. I have not been able to break 128 pounds when my ideal weight is 150–155 pounds. Some journey, huh?

Well, the one thing I don't want is for people to feel sorry for me. I don't feel sorry for myself, and neither should you. Life is hard, and you never know what it's going to throw at you! Sometimes, things happen for a reason! The Bible says God works in mysterious ways, and man, do I believe it. You see, I could have come up with all kinds of excuses as to why I couldn't reach the pinnacle of success: my health and having to take care of my younger brother with my parents, which, believe me, is a daily struggle. We have not had a peaceful day in our house for over ten years. When my parents pass away, I will have to take care of my younger brother all by myself. I never got married or into a serious relationship because I thought it would be unfair to bring anybody else into my problems!

In life, you have to learn how to turn your negative situations into positive ones. So, how did I turn this into a positive situation? Simple. What drives me to reach the top of the success ladder is knowing I will be able to take care of my brother when my parents pass away. I want to be able to give him everything he wants and deserves in life. Even though he is a pain in the you-know-what to deal with, I know deep down inside that he is a sweet human being with a big heart. He was dealt a bad hand in having severe mental issues that I wouldn't wish on my worst enemies. Trust me, my medical problems are nothing compared to what he has and is still going through! So, that's the number one reason that drives me to be successful.

What's the other one? It's to show the whole world that no matter what you are going through, you have the innate ability to accomplish whatever you want in life. Don't let obstacles stop you from fulfilling your dreams. *Please* don't be afraid to dream big! The bigger, the better! How does the saying go: Go big or go home? So why not go big? As stated in the movie *Rudy*, dreams are what make life tolerable. Without dreams, life kinda sucks! I've always told myself I'm either going to be a bum or one of the most successful people you will ever meet. There is no in-between for me. Either I will make it to the top of the mountain of success, or you'll find me dead on the side of it, from trying to reach the top with all my heart! That's the attitude you must have when it comes to fulfilling your dreams. You only live one life, correct? Shouldn't you try to make it the best of it? You can't let obstacles, and especially fear, stand in your way.

I'm going to tell you it won't be easy. You're going to fail many times—as *all* successful people have. I know this because I have failed more times than most people. But I believe in failing forward and not backward. There is nothing in this world that will stop me from fulfilling my dreams because they mean the world to me, as yours should to you!

Just remember that to be successful, your mind has to be like a parachute: it must have the ability to open up! What does that mean? It means you're going to have to look at things differently than the average person. It means you're probably going to have to do some things that make you uncomfortable at first. Embrace the uncomfortable feelings because they will go away eventually; doing the task at hand will become second nature! And lastly, please pay attention to who you listen to in life. In my profession, many people fail, but many succeed! The difference for me was that I surrounded myself with the ones who succeeded. Why would I listen to people who have failed at something when I have a burning desire to be successful at the very same thing? It makes no sense. So, be sure you take advice from people who have the same goals and desires as you!

I hope what I have said resonates with all of you. I want you all to know that success, no doubt, means having nice cars, houses, jewelry, vacations, etc. But those are all secondary to me. What excites me the most about massive success is the ability to take care of my brother and contribute to society as much as I can by donating large sums of money to organizations such as the ASPCA, Wounded Warrior Project, St. Jude's, the Kidney Foundation, to our veterans, mental health organizations, and many, many more! I have made a commitment to myself that from now until they put me six feet under, I am going to assist as many people as I can, health-wise and economically. I was lucky enough to find the vehicle to do so and with the most incredible mentor I could ever ask for! By the way, finding a great mentor is key to your success, which is why I am using my business platform as a stepping stone to reach my real dream, which is to become a motivational speaker.

So, here's to success in everything we do. If I can help out in any way, shape, or form, please come and find me. I promise I will do everything in my power to help make your dreams become a reality. Whatever your mind conceives and believes, it can achieve!

BIOGRAPHY

Vineet Bhardwaj has spent the last fifteen years learning from the best motivational speakers in the industry. He has worked directly with coaches from The Tony Robbins Foundation to attending seminars by John Maxwell, Jack Canfield, Tony Robbins, Mel Robbins, Sir Richard Branson, the late Sean Stevenson, and many others, which lit a fire in him to become an author and a future motivational speaker himself. He has taken several courses through The Napoleon Hill Foundation and is an affiliate with the company. He is highly motivated to take what he has learned and pass it onto others so they can live the life of their dreams. His passion for helping people shows with his constant and positive attitude towards life, no matter what negative obstacles come his way. He is a sincere, kind, and loving individual with a huge heart who wishes nothing but the best for people and what they wish to accomplish in their lives.

Connect with Vineet Bhardwaj via https://linktr.ee/vbcharger11

The End

www.ingramcontent.com/pod-product-compliance
Lightning Source LLC
Chambersburg PA
CBHW021402210526
45463CB00001B/192